The Joseph Dialogues

Also by Alan Sorem

Lucy Scott's Grand Stand;
Age Is an Attitude,
Not a Condition

Two other novels in
The Holy Family trilogy:

Time: Jesus in Relationships
The Rabbi's Daughter

The Joseph Dialogues

A novel

Alan Sorem

RESOURCE *Publications* · Eugene, Oregon

THE JOSEPH DIALOGUES
A novel

Resource Publications
An Imprint of Wipf and Stock Publishers
199 W. 8th Ave., Suite 3
Eugene, OR 97401

www.wipfandstock.com

ISBN 13: 978-1-4982-3835-9

Manufactured in the U.S.A.   12/02/2015

With thanksgiving to God
for the lives of my brother,
David Nelson Sorem
1934–2012,
and his son, my nephew,
Jeffery Nelson Sorem
1960–2015.

Fides et Fortis

1

I am still in shock from the news. A week ago Joseph visited me in southern Syria. There was the usual purchase of lumber. Today a traveler from the south brought word of Joseph's funeral yesterday in Nazareth.

My dear friend, a man I regarded as a brother, is gone. I cannot control my legs, my arms, my whole body from shaking. Our conversations about politics, religion, and lumber—abruptly ended. "Dialogues" he called them, smiling as he pronounced the word.

Oh, Joseph. Why have you left me? Where is there justice in a God who would do such a thing!

Mere days ago my energetic and robust friend took his leave in the late afternoon. My warning about the storm clouds building behind Mount Hermon fell on deaf ears. Delighted at the price we had agreed on for a cartload of quality cedar, he was eager to get it home to his carpentry shop in Nazareth. He had a commission for a fishing vessel and the time line was short even with the help of his sons. I assisted him with his first hull. In the forty or more years since, fishing vessels always brought a gleam to his eyes.

Forty years of friendship.

I have aged today. My housekeeper brought me my cane when I could not stand without it. But Joseph, still young even as he approached his sixtieth birthday, possessed the exuberance and outlook of a much younger man. In his last conversation with me he spoke of new possibilities for his family and his trade.

I will hold my right hand with my left this evening to calm it so that I can lift a cup of my finest wine to toast him.

Until I met Joseph I held no religious beliefs at all except the worth of Roman coins in my cash box. Roman, Greek, Jewish gods—what value do they have in the marketplace?

Yet Joseph was my dear friend. A week ago I urged him to stay the night as usual. As enticement I offered good wine and fresh lamb prepared by my housekeeper.

We both enjoyed the dialogues we had that often lasted into the late evening. We were two men of a world much larger than the small villages in which we lived. His trade took him throughout Galilee, and he was familiar with Jerusalem and Alexandria as well. I knew the sights and streets of Damascus and of Tyre on the coast. As a youth, with my father and older brothers, I had visited cities much farther north: Antioch and the metropolis of Ephesus, for example.

I anticipated another evening of good conversation that day a week ago. But no, even though it was already late afternoon, this one time he was eager to be on the road to Nazareth with his prized cargo.

I looked to the south and cautioned him. Dark clouds were mounting up that threatened to spill over Mount Hermon and bring heavy rainfall to Galilee. He laughed at my fears and said he would push the horse to a fast trot and be home with Mary and his children that night.

And so he went on with a final wave as he turned from the lane onto the main road.

He did not outrun the chilling rain that fell. By the time he reached Nazareth he had a hoarse cough and took to bed immediately. Within the week he was dead, the traveler told me. In the telling, the traveler's eyes were moist and his words halting. For him, too, Joseph had been a good friend.

I urged the messenger to stay a night so that we might commiserate together, but he was bound for Antioch and wanted to move along.

Joseph is gone and what I write expresses my deep sorrow. To honor our friendship I feel I must do something more.

I will write about our dialogues in the evenings we had together.

2

Joseph's carpenter father first approached me in the year that the Senate in Rome named Octavian "Imperator Caesar Divi Filius Augustus." Fine Latin words that are meaningless to those who are far from Rome. Our trade in the prosperous regions of the East continues to be conducted in Greek; those who pride themselves on bilingual excellence tell me that the words mean "Emperor Caesar Augustus the Divine Son." We knew him simply by his Greek name, Sebastos.

Other than recurring tax levies, the affairs of Rome in those days caused few ripples for us on the eastern shore of the Great Sea. From Rome, Augustus controlled Egypt and other wealthy lands in North Africa. As Julius Caesar's stepson he had inherited two-thirds of the assassinated emperor's wealth. In every crisis he had ample funds to resolve matters quickly. In the West, the Iberian tribes were a recent conquest. The concerns of ever-expansive Rome at the time I write involve battles for conquest of the Germanic tribes along the Rhine.

For men of our times, destiny was determined at birth. I grow and sell timber, as did a host of ancestors that stretch back to a military man, Demostrate, who cut trees and constructed bridges for Alexander and his army along his long march of conquest.

What is known and revered in family lore is this: when Alexander died in the East and his army made their way back to Macedonia, Demostrate chose to settle along the way, as did many others. He purchased land in the south of the province of Syria, land filled with trees valuable for woodworking—cedar, cypress, poplar, oak, and olive.

For fourteen generations of sons with Greek names, we have been wood merchants. Illness took my two older brothers and now I, Alexios, am the final son in this trade. It will end with me. Years ago my beloved Sophia died in childbirth, as did my stillborn son. My heart has never found joy in the thought of marrying another. The family trade will end with me.

But I digress.

For some time now I have been the premier tree farmer in the southern part of Syria. My laborers prune my trees carefully, and they are beautiful to behold as they grow strong and true. For every tree I cut, two are planted to assure a continuing supply. It was no surprise to me that Joseph's father, a Jew from Galilee in the South, would hear of me as he searched for wood of a superior quality.

He was nearing sixty when we met. Cheerful of countenance, he was a simple, honest man who did not dicker over prices, a great difference from others who visited my storehouses of hewn cedar and cypress and other woods. We'd reach a point in the sale at which he would clap his hands, beam at me, and exclaim, "That's that, then."

I believe it was on his fifth annual trip that his son accompanied him, a young man in his twenties.

"My only child," his father said, smiling, "but the Lord has been gracious to me. Joseph has the strength of three men and the wisdom of four."

The next year Joseph came alone and I learned the truth of the first part of his father's words. It was a day when no laborers were present to load the long horse cart. Once we had reached agreement on the price, Joseph proceeded to pull the trimmed and bucksaw-hewn trunks from their bins onto a loading table. He found the midpoint of each one, grunted, lifted, and slowly proceeded to the nearby cart. When he had loaded the last tree trunk in the cart, he turned and laughed at my amazement.

"In my other work, I help carry stones from quarry to cart for a friend."

Not for several more visits did he accept my invitation to stay the night and become better acquainted over cups of fine wine.

3

On the day of Joseph's sixth annual visit, as usual in early spring of the year, the choice of woods lasted into early afternoon so that loading of the cart took longer than usual. On this occasion, he accepted my invitation to stay the night.

We dined on chicken and sliced vegetables from the garden. My housekeeper washed up and left us with another jar of wine. We moved to more comfortable chairs near the hearth. The evenings were cool and a fire had been lighted earlier.

There was a matter I had been thinking about since his last visit. I leaned toward him after we had dispensed with idle chatter.

"My friend, you need a wife," I told him bluntly.

He laughed. "Alexios, such a sudden change to a serious subject."

"I have been thinking. You are in the same situation that I find myself. My brothers had no children. Nor do I. It is time to marry and have children."

"We shall both be rude," he responded. "What you suggest seems more suited to yourself. You are older than I by at least ten more years." He smiled to take the bite from his words. "Less time to be a father."

I leaned back in my chair and raised my cup of wine to him.

"Ah, but I *was* married. To a beautiful, wonderful woman. We were to have a child, but her heart was not strong enough for a long delivery. Our son died with her."

Joseph stared at me. "I am so sorry to hear of this. My father never mentioned it."

"It was before he came to me." I shrugged. "I have made my peace with the life I have and do not wish to search for another wife."

"There is yet time for a son and heir. Or several sons."

"No. For me a housekeeper is sufficient. She makes excellent meals at a reasonable cost, keeps the house clean, and washes my clothes when needed. She never argues with me about anything and returns to her own family at the end of the day, leaving me in peace."

I turned the issue back to him.

"Surely your father has spoken of this marriage matter?"

"Yes." He turned his gaze to the logs in the hearth that gave us warmth from their ruddy embers. "It seems a more pressing matter for you."

I laughed. "To find someone whose only duty is to produce a son? Is that what I am to do?"

"Alexios!"

"That is the relationship you suggest. For the sake of a possible son or sons to carry on the work?" I snorted. "It would not be fair to the woman! In my heart I still mourn my Sophia."

Joseph was silent.

I pressed him again. "Surely in Nazareth or elsewhere in Galilee there is a woman for you who will bring you the joy of many children."

"My father has spoken of this."

"Has he been more specific? Names?"

Joseph laughed and turned to me. "Once or twice he has said to me, 'Pass by the town well today at midday and watch for the one who curtsies to you.'"

"And what has come of this?"

"Nothing but girls giggling as I pass by."

"No curtsy?"

"Oh, yes, but well hidden in the flock of gigglers."

"Hmm. I think your father should be more definite."

Joseph's eyes turned to survey the fire in the hearth. "My mother presses him. I sometimes hear them speaking of it." After a pause, he said, "You still have time for a son. Or sons."

I stood and grasped the tongs by the hearth and settled the logs.

"I will get a good price for my land and trees. One day. But you, an only son. A son in his twenties. Surely you have sufficient means by now to afford a wife."

I turned back to him but he avoided my eyes.

"There is not always harmony in my house," he said.

"Your father is a man of good cheer."

"Indeed. A man innocent of malice. He is not the problem."

"A common story," I remarked and returned to my chair.

"Yes."

I glanced at him. "That is why I cannot think of anyone taking Sophia's place. She was a delight! But enough of old tales. Tell me about the disharmony."

"My father, like you, would have preferred many sons. They did not come. He has difficulty now with carpentry measurements. More and more he leaves the work to me and finds pleasure in sitting in the sunshine of the garden and musing about old times."

"And your mother?"

"My mother desired daughters as handmaidens to serve her every wish. They did not come. And now she is past the age for bearing children. She has turned sour and resentful and would be a burden on any bride of mine."

"And you, Joseph? What do you wish for?"

He thought for a moment, eyeing the floor, and then spoke quietly. "An intelligent girl, one who has household skills, but one who can truly be a loving partner just as you describe your Sophia." He paused. "Peace in the house would be nice also."

"Ah."

"And it is a complicated matter." He looked at me. "Have you the custom here—when the bride marries she goes to her husband's house?"

"Depends on what money they have."

8

"For us it is always. The men in the bride's family keep the family's income intact. The man's family pays the bride-price. The woman comes to their house."

"It is a different arrangement here. How much is the bride-price?"

"In Nazareth, usually four hundred shekels or so for a virgin. Less for a widow." Joseph grimaced. "But I cannot imagine a woman who would wish to marry me and be under the thumb of my mother."

"Perhaps the price paid may need to be higher."

"Yes. Nazareth is a small village. The families are well acquainted with each other. I cannot imagine a woman who would be my wife for less than five or six hundred. Or more," he added.

I nodded in agreement. "As is said, two women in a house often are one too many."

Joseph sighed. "That is certainly true in my mother's case."

"So, shall you wait until they are gone and you are free to choose?"

He gave me a long look and then replied. "I have thought of that."

"But your father, though older, seems energetic still. Your mother may be so, as well. It could be quite some time. And you, have you no desire for the comfort and closeness of a woman?"

He smiled. "I prefer my own company at present."

We both turned our eyes to the hearth and watched the flames licking at the logs for a while.

"And you," Joseph asked at last, "have you no desire for the comfort and closeness of a woman?"

A sudden vision of Sophia bloomed in my mind. A day when we had gone walking in the countryside and she slowed and turned to me, her face radiant as she told me that she was with child. A joyful day. I had suppressed all memory of that day for long years since her death. My eyes filled with tears.

"Alexios?"

I wiped my eyes. "A sudden memory," I replied huskily.

"Sophia?"

"Three years we had together. Wonderful years."

I smiled. "My father wanted me to marry a younger girl in town. He told me, 'She has the build fit for a mother of many children.' But I had glimpsed another woman in the marketplace. I had seen her as she picked out fruit. A lovely smile, a slim build, and such beautiful dark hair she had, coiled respectably under her headscarf. I knew at once that we were meant for each other. I learned of her name from the fruit seller. Sophia. A friend spoke to her father.

"Another memory. How delighted she was early in our courtship at my gift to her of a hair comb carved from olive wood. She danced around me, laughing with excitement as she waved the comb in her hand. Then she handed the comb to me and said. 'You must be the first to comb my hair with this.' With that she pulled off her scarf, loosened several pins, and her lovely long hair tumbled almost to her waist. It was the day of our first kiss."

I turned to Joseph, my eyes moist. "Imagine! A woman in her twenties, passed over for whatever reason by others. Soon to be considered a spinster, only good for service as an aunt to the children of her brothers and sisters."

Joseph smiled. "But saved for you. I remember a verse of the Psalmist. 'You have put gladness in my heart, more than when grain and wine and oil increase.'"

"Yes, great gladness for each other and a deep love I had never dreamed possible." My voice grew husky. "Three years—"

I could not speak further.

Joseph leaned over to me and put a hand on my shoulder and spoke softly.

"Alexios, better than no years at all."

"Not true! To have the warmth of love and partnership. To wake with joy every morning knowing that once again I would see her dear face, and then, gone! Never to see her again! It is a living death for me!"

"Is this what you believe?"

"Yes."

"I think a different way."

Sudden anger rose in me and I glared at him.

"Yes, you Jews have your God to comfort you! Mind the Commandments you have been given and the sacrifices and burnt offerings that you make to appease your God! Follow the rules and enter the heavenly kingdom. A fool's dream! Empty words of consolation, I say!"

Joseph spoke quietly. "I believe you will see Sophia again."

With an edge to my voice I said, "Is this your way of consoling me? Stop."

His soft voice continued. "Please do not be offended."

"What rubbish!" I wanted to slap him and shake his whole frame for such talk. Instead I pulled his hand from my shoulder and turned my face away.

"Alexios, death is real. When I think of my own mortality, at times I am frightened of the darkness that may come and feel powerless. But there is something other than the Law and the Commandments that gives me hope in times when hope seems impossible."

I turned back to face him with scorn in my voice. "So, are you among those who consult the witches and seek news of the departed?"

"No, never! My hope comes from a prophet of old named Micah. In a time when my people were trodden down by the rich and powerful, he said many things, but of them all, one saying is inscribed on my heart: 'What does the Lord require of you? To do justice, to love kindness, and to walk humbly with your God.'"

"Huh!" I snorted, "A fine notion."

"Alexios, I know you find no worth in Roman gods."

"The belief of fools. With every conquest Rome adds local gods to the list and thus soothes the conquered people."

We both looked at the hearth. There were no words between us for a time. When at last Joseph spoke again it was in a low voice.

"You think me young, but I, too, have endured much."

"Then be satisfied with your faith and may it comfort you in hard times."

"I offer these words as comfort for you also."

"Oh, are you now to convert me? So that I may worship in your synagogue and rock myself to and fro as I stand in prayer to the invisible one you call your Lord?"

"Alexios, I come here to purchase excellent wood, not to make you into someone you have no desire to be."

"Thank you."

"In my visits of these past years I have come to know you."

"And I you. Up to now we have been comfortable together."

"May it continue. What seem to be boundaries may not be so."

"Meaning?"

Joseph looked me full in the face.

"Without knowing the prophet Micah you follow the path of his words. You are a just man, a kind man. I believe your love for Sophia and hers for you does not end in the grave. Your love will be recognized."

"We are born; we die." I responded. "That is the beginning and the end of our existence."

"It is not. Think of your love for her, your memories of her. Neither has ended."

"Words, words," I muttered.

"Love is greater than death, Alexios."

"We must stick to what the eye can see and the ear can hear."

Joseph paused. I was waiting for more words of the scripture he studied. I would rebut it as well, I told myself. But he surprised me.

"Alexios, tell me. You truly loved Sophia and truly love her still?"

"Don't be silly. Of course."

"Of course. Now think with me for a moment. When we have spoken of the Lord, you picture God as an angry, wrathful god, a god who must be appeased. A god we weak humans never can live up to. Am I right?"

"Somewhat. My belief is that we have only ourselves for help."

"I understand. But what if, instead of an aloof, easily angered god, there is a Lord who has created all that is, and loves us and wants the very best for us. What you wanted for Sophia."

"Yes," I said softly. "And she was taken from me. Is that the kind of love your Lord shows us?"

He was silent, thinking. At last he spoke once more.

"There was a time when the people cried out to heaven in anguish. The prophet Isaiah spoke the word of the Lord to them. 'Do not fear, for I am with you. I will help you. I will uphold you with my right hand, my hand of righteousness.'"

We looked at each other for some time. I was the first to turn away.

My eyes had dried. I felt a stirring of hope within me as well as a deep fatigue. I had not spoken of Sophia for years, and the sudden onrush of memories overwhelmed me.

"Perhaps," I said. I rose. "But let us not argue the matter further. A good night's sleep will prepare you for your journey home."

"I bid you a good night also," Joseph replied.

We went to our separate beds in silence. As I extinguished the oil lamp on my bedside table, I spoke words into the darkness that I had not used since that last night before her birth pains began.

"Good night, my darling. Rest well."

For the first time in many months, my sleep was dreamless.

After a simple breakfast in the morning, I invited Joseph to walk with me to the tallest cypress in my land of trees. It is where Sophia's face was bright with joy as she told me she was with child. She and our son are buried there.

We stood there silently for a time, Joseph and I. My anger and resentment of the night before had softened. I asked him to say a few words from his own tradition. He offered a brief prayer of thanksgiving for Sophia's life.

"Eternal Lord, we thank you for the life of Sophia. When sadness threatens to overcome Alexios, remind him that she and the child are held close in your everlasting care, free from pain in glorious light along with others we have loved. To you we ascribe all honor and glory forever. So be it."

Our arms around each other's shoulders, I walked with him to his horse and loaded cart. Simple words of farewell and he was on his way back to Nazareth.

As my hand lowered from a final wave of parting, I realized that Joseph accepted me and came to me not only as a buyer of wood but also as a true friend.

4

The summer that followed was exceptionally busy and I had few further thoughts of Joseph until the winter lull set in. It was a time when I made visits to every section of my woodland to make notes of the new plantings my laborers would make in the spring.

I also noted the trees that were ready for harvesting. One in particular was a great oak that an ancestor long generations ago had planted. It was a magnificent tree, towering above those around it. But it also blocked sunlight from younger trees, and I had decided that it was time to bring the great oak down.

In the early years the oak had been tended well. The resulting trunk was thick and even up to a considerable height, and as I surveyed it, the thought of Joseph and the construction of large wheels for huge carts sprang to my mind. I smiled at the thought and it remained with me through the winter months. How pleased he would be when he heard my proposal!

The days turned warmer at last. A message came with a traveler going north. Joseph expected to be with me in three days time.

The weather continued warm and the blooms of spring were all around. I asked my housekeeper to prepare midday meal packets for Joseph and me on the day he was to arrive.

He came. We made our usual visit to the storehouse and soon his order list was fulfilled. It was barely midday as he turned to me.

"Quick work on a lovely day." He smiled. "I may as well make for home."

"Indeed it is a lovely day. I have a diversion for us to enjoy this afternoon."

"Oh?"

"Yes. We have packets from my housekeeper with delights for our midday meal. I have two secrets of the land to show you. We can see the first and then enjoy our meal in the pleasant surroundings of the second."

"Intriguing," smiled Joseph. "I will stay."

Within a short time I had hoisted a backpack over my shoulders that contained our food as well as a flask of wine. I pointed to a trail we had not traveled previously.

"That way."

As we walked along the pathway deeper into the woods, I chatted with Joseph about the types of carts he constructed and the wheels they required. What would he do with a larger cart than one known in Galilee? A cart on which a houseful of new furniture might be carried. Our conversation continued until we were about to reach the great oak, its trunk hidden behind smaller oaks.

I paused and he stopped beside me.

"I am going to show you something very special. But I want it to be a surprise. So, give me your hand and close your eyes and I will lead you to it."

Joseph gave me a quizzical glance but followed my instructions. I led him off the pathway to a clearing from which the great oak was clearly visible.

"Now," I prompted, "open your eyes."

His eyes opened and opened further. The majesty of the great oak was amazing.

"I have never seen such a tree," he breathed.

We walked closer.

"How many centuries?" he asked.

"Nearly four, according to the records I have."

He walked ahead and began to circle the tree.

"And the careful pruning," he remarked, "scarcely noticeable."

"Yes, pruned from an early age so that the trunk is clear and straight quite a ways up."

He reached my side again. "An amazing specimen."

I nodded. "I have decided to cut it down soon, and I was wondering . . ."

"Seems a shame."

"It is a unique oak. The breadth of the trunk may be well suited to special applications in carpentry."

"Oh?" Joseph's eyes were focused on the trunk.

"I was wondering if you think it possible to have fully formed wheels from one cutting of the trunk."

He pursed his lips. "It is possible. They would be huge." He laughed. "The topic of our conversation." He turned to me. "Each one all of a single piece?"

"Yes. Can you think of ways such wheels might be used?"

"Such a cart surely would be larger than anything I have seen. And it would require at least two horses."

"To be used by a quarry, perhaps?"

"Yes. In the proposed building of the new Temple in Jerusalem. Or in further construction in Herod's new seaport, Caesarea Maritima."

"Exactly."

Joseph turned to me. "You can cut such wheels?"

"I think so. It will require precision once the tree is hewn. Of course, the upper limbs would be cut before the tree is brought down."

Joseph frowned and I could see him calculating.

"Have you any idea of the price of such a wheel?"

I named a price. He sucked a breath in as he turned to survey the trunk again.

"You would do the cutting?" he asked.

"Yes. The smoothing is for you to do. And mounting the metal rims."

He nodded and murmured, "I would need at least two sets of four similar wheels." He turned to me again. "For two carts. But I cannot pay you until I have sold the completed carts. If I can find buyers."

"I understand. If you give me a tenth of the payment beforehand, I will accept the balance later."

"I need to think about who may need such vehicles. Someone near good Roman roads."

17

"Of course." I looked upward at the trunk. "I estimate I can easily get six sets of four wheels if the cutting is done by careful measurement. Perhaps more."

We spoke a bit longer, but I was eager to take him onward to my next surprise. Soon we were on the pathway again.

The land rose as we walked. Through a stand of poplars I glimpsed the small hill ahead that was our destination.

"Just a bit more," I said. "I think you will enjoy what you are about to see."

The pathway circled to the left and came up over a rise. We stopped.

"Incredible!" Joseph exclaimed.

We were standing on a low shoulder of the hill that sloped downward to an expansive pool of clear water.

He turned to me. "But where does the water come from?"

I smiled. "The pool is fed from an underground stream which has never run dry. But come, there is a place," I pointed, "where we will have shade as we enjoy our midday meal."

As we ate the contents of our packets and drank wine from the flask, I told Joseph a treasured family story. Long ago the pool was the reason Demostrate purchased the land.

"Therefore it is called Demostrate's Pool," I explained. "In the summer, children from the village come and swim. I insist at least one adult must accompany them, as the pool deepens considerably near the middle."

We chatted on and at last I asked Joseph a question.

"I know your father. You have told me about your mother and things about Nazareth. But your name is not a common one in our area. How did you come by it?"

"My name? Joseph, you mean?"

"Yes. Those who live here are descendants of Greeks and the old names are passed down. But that is not true in Galilee."

"Only a few Greek names, it is true. But Joseph is an honorable name, and there are other Josephs in Galilee."

We were sitting on the grass and he turned to me.

"You have never heard of the famous Joseph of Hebrew heritage?"

"No. Was he a famous king?"

"Not quite. But let me tell you the amazing story of Joseph."

5

"Joseph," he began, "was the eleventh son of a man named Jacob. The first by Jacob's wife Rachel. In his youth, Jacob's mother had connived with him to cheat his older brother, Esau, out of his inheritance. But that is a story for another time. The important thing to know is that Joseph was the darling child of Jacob. He received many gifts from his father. As he grew older, Joseph's older brothers were jealous to the point of boiling anger. And it did boil over one day as they all were tending flocks."

It sounded to me like an old Greek tale. "They killed him!"

"No. They wanted to, but the oldest brother, Reuben, convinced them to dig a pit instead and leave Joseph there to die."

"Did he?"

Joseph smiled. "No. Others came along, helped him out of the pit and sold him to the head of a camel caravan that passed by."

"This is a true story?"

"It is a true story."

"So the caravan ended up somewhere and he was sold again."

Joseph nodded. "Yes. Egypt. And he was sold to the captain of Pharaoh's guards. He became a very able manager of the household. The captain's wife desired Joseph, but he refused her advances."

"Ah. There is no anger as hot as that of a spurned woman."

"Exactly. She told her husband a lie. Joseph was the one who made advances and he forcibly took her."

"So it was 'goodbye Joseph.'"

"Indeed. Off to jail, where an interesting thing happened. Joseph's skill in handling matters was readily apparent. The chief jailer gave Joseph authority over all the prisoners."

"They broke out?"

"Oh, no. Something else. Two important members of the royal household—the chief cupbearer and the chief baker—offended Pharaoh and were thrown in the same prison."

"And they schemed with Joseph."

My Joseph laughed. "Wrong again. The two disgraced men had strange dreams, which Joseph interpreted for them." He held up his hand to forestall my next comment. "The dreams, he told them, meant that in three days the chief cupbearer was to be restored to his position but the chief baker was to be hanged. And so it came about."

"This tale has many twists and turns."

"Yes. But then for quite a while nothing further happened as Joseph continued in his role as manager of the prisoners."

"And then?"

My friend smiled. "Two years later, Pharaoh had strange dreams. First about seven sleek and fat cows and a second one about seven lean and ugly cows. Pharaoh fretted and fussed about the meaning of the dreams, but neither he nor anyone in his court could make sense of them. At last the cupbearer remembered Joseph and told Pharaoh of a man who had interpreted his own dream."

"Aha. Joseph goes to the Pharaoh's palace."

"Yes. And he told Pharaoh the meaning of the dreams. Seven good years of crops were coming, followed by seven years of famine. For the Egyptians to survive, huge storehouses needed to be built, to be filled by crops from the seven bountiful years."

"I can see it all. Joseph was placed in charge of building the storehouses."

"Even better." My friend gave me a broad grin. "He became the governor over the land at the right hand of Pharaoh."

I clapped my hands. "What a good ending for the boy thrown into a pit by jealous brothers!"

"Oh, but there is more."

"Still more? Is this a Jewish version of Odysseus?"

"Please, Alexios, patience."

I leaned back on the grassy slope. "Continue."

"When the famine came, it was widespread. It even affected Joseph's homeland. The storehouses held so much grain that Pharaoh offered aid to lands beyond Egypt.

"In time the ten older brothers of Joseph came as supplicants, bowing to a regal figure whom they did not recognize in his majestic robes. But he recognized them and developed a plan. He accused them of being spies, which, of course, they denied. One brother was to be kept as prisoner until they returned with the youngest brother, Benjamin. Before they left, they were allowed a generous share of bags of grain. Joseph instructed his men secretly to place inside each bag at the top the payments made."

I smiled. "And when they discovered this, they were terrified."

"Yes. But they were safely home. Except for that brother left as prisoner."

"And when all the grain they had been given was gone?"

"Heavy hearts. Jacob, their father, said they must return to Egypt, taking a double payment and other gifts. And young Benjamin, his twelfth son, born of the same mother as Joseph."

"They walked into a trap."

"So it seemed," he replied. "But at first they were treated well and given more grain to take home, but again their payments—doubled now—were placed in the bags, and, in the bag of Benjamin, Joseph's silver cup was placed."

"Oh, dear."

"At Joseph's urging the steward hastened after them and accused them of theft, which, of course, they again denied. The bags were opened and they were horrified. They were taken back to meet an angry Joseph, and they pleaded to be made slaves as recompense. Joseph refused, telling them that only Benjamin would be made a slave. At this, a brother named Judah stepped forward and told him that Benjamin's brother, Joseph, had died and pleaded that the loss also of Benjamin would kill their father."

"Surely this melted Joseph's anger?"

"Yes. He ordered everyone else from the room and he revealed himself to them. There were many tears from all eyes."

"Ah, a happy ending."

"Even better. Joseph invited everyone in the extended family to come and settle in Egypt. They did so and were given the best of land."

My friend fell silent.

"What a lovely ending!" I exclaimed.

"For many years it was so." He sighed. "In later years a Pharaoh arose who did not know the story. The people were enslaved."

"I know something of the story. Perhaps your Joseph became too thoroughly an Egyptian. The one who was protector did not pass on his mantle of protection."

"Perhaps." He turned to me with saddened eyes. "You have heard of Moses?"

"I know he led your ancestors out of Egyptian slavery into your present land."

"Even more. He was the one who gave the Lord's Law to us. I could tell you many things about Moses, but the most important thing for me comes from his charge to the Hebrew people as they were about to enter the new land.

"'Hear, O Israel: The Lord is our God, the Lord alone. You shall love the Lord your God with all your heart, and with all your soul, and with all your might. Keep these words that I am commanding you today in your heart. Recite them to your children and talk about them when you are at home and when you are away, when you lie down and when you rise.'

"I will follow this instruction with my children, if I am so blessed."

"I can well believe that you will." I nodded. "It seems like a great deal of work!"

"It is at the heart of who I am, Alexios."

"Yes, of course. But back to your story about Joseph. It does not explain to me why your father gave you the name."

"He has never said." Joseph laughed. "Perhaps he thought I was to rise to a higher position than carpenter. Or to have dreams—and to be able to interpret them."

He looked at me. "Your turn now. Tell me of your own name and the ancestors in the family."

We remained at the pool for several hours. It was a delightful time and a memory I treasure.

6

A year passed. There were many carpenters who sought the wood of my trees, but I found my thoughts turning to the last visit of Joseph. Now that we had become closer, I wanted to see him settled with a good wife.

I was glad when winter turned to spring. Soon he would return. He did.

I quizzed him as we settled into comfortable chairs after the evening meal.

"May I ask again about prospects for marriage?"

Joseph laughed. "Surely you have not made this your only concern?"

"No. But today your talk of successful projects—you must have ample means for marriage now."

"Early days, my friend, early days."

"You are not so reticent, as a rule."

Joseph smiled. "The news from the south is that King Herod has begun to rebuild the Temple in Jerusalem. There had been rumors of it. Now it is happening."

"I drink to his health that he may last the years needed to finish it."

"Herod has promised that the Temple itself will be finished quickly. He has architects and stonemasons from many parts of Roman rule. The Temple priests themselves will be involved in the actual construction of the Temple building. When can a number of larger wheels be ready?"

"I have a sampling behind the tool house as a surprise for you."

"Good. I have a buyer—the quarry master in Jerusalem. I have brought you the down payment you mentioned. I will be able to pay you the remainder on my next visit."

I lifted my cup again. "Excellent! I drink to your continued success so that you may pay the hefty taxes which doubtless will be levied."

"And how are matters here?" he asked.

"Our imperial governor, Sentius Saturninus, has been succeeded by a man named Varus. He arrived in the company of three Roman legions. You surely noticed that my charges for your purchased wood are higher. We have felt the weight of increased taxes."

"I assumed as much."

"You have new levies imposed for the reconstruction of the Temple?"

"I am sure they will be assessed, but thus far only the usual tax for those who attend religious festivals in Jerusalem during the year. Other widespread levies have increased under King Herod to pay for the building of Caesarea Maritima, the seaport where he now resides, and for Masada and the Herodium, his hill fortresses."

I nodded. "The taxes here had been stable until the arrival of Varus and his imposition of new emergency taxes. The roads must be improved by his decree; levies have increased on the sale of grain, fruit, and lumber. One never knows what the future holds. The censor holds the tax rights over all. New bidders may arise for the taxation rights for lesser districts, and that will mean extra amounts imposed by the regional collectors down to the local ones."

Joseph nodded. "We are fortunate in Nazareth. We have an honest and straightforward tax collector."

"Come now, such a man does not exist!"

"He has a meeting once a year with the town householders, and another with the farmers in our district."

"A time for groaning at the increased charges?"

"Not at all. He reviews the base of all the taxes for the coming season, the amount he has paid to secure his position, and the amount added by him for the upkeep of his family and home. The last part—his amount—is regarded as reasonable in Nazareth."

"A marvel!"

"Indeed. The result is that we have lower taxes than other districts around us. And his position is secure. Over the years there were other men who wished to capture the position by offering a larger bribe to the regional publican. Their efforts were nullified by public protests."

"And the publican? Where does he stand?"

"He values peace in our district rather than protests." Joseph smiled. "In an earlier year, he actually named another man tax collector. We learned the choice meant a large increase in our taxes, an obvious result of the sum paid to secure the position. The publican retracted his choice after our farmers dumped two cartloads of manure in front of his house."

"I wish our farmers were as brave."

"You have three Roman legions stationed nearby."

I grimaced. "Yes, a sizable deterrent to protests."

"And the wonder of wonders is that our man worships in the synagogue and no eyebrows are raised or muffled sneers heard."

I raised my cup. "Here is to your tax collector."

"May it continue to be so," he replied, and we drained our cups.

I rose to fetch the ewer and poured more wine.

"I trust you have noticed the higher quality of wine this year?"

"Yes. The lumber business has prospered?"

"Despite higher taxes, yes. And you?"

"An increase in chests, tables, and the like in home furnishings. The good harvest of last summer brought more orders for field sledges, carts, and plows to prepare the fields for the next sowing."

"Ah. An opportune time to return to the forbidden topic."

"My marriage, you mean." He laughed. "As a matter of fact, there have been feelers."

"A local girl you know?"

"No. One from the village of Cana. A kinsman who now lives in Nazareth has been the go-between."

He sipped his wine.

"Please," I urged. "More details."

"She is daughter of the rabbi in Cana. She is an only child, as am I. We have met and the bride-price my father must pay seems reasonable."

"Does she suit your requirements?"

"Mary is much younger than your Sophia when you married, but from our conversation I judge her to be intelligent and quite knowledgeable about household matters."

"A partner, as you wish?"

"She has sparkling eyes and an even temperament that will bode well with my mother. In a brief conversation while walking the streets of Cana, I learned that she desires many children, as I do. And she is good with numbers. I hope for her to keep my accounts in order."

"Goodness, you have done well!"

Joseph smiled broadly. "Yes. Some matter has arisen lately that her parents wish to discuss with my parents and me, but I have put off a visit from them until I return. Her father is a straight-forward man who is careful about small details, and it cannot be anything of great importance. The betrothal has been announced in both our villages, and all that remains is to set a date soon for the wedding."

Again I lifted my wine cup. "I congratulate you and wish you well."

"Thank you, my friend. Once a date has been set I will send word to you. Your attendance on that occasion would please me greatly."

"I will be honored to do so."

We spoke of other things until we finished the wine. I was delighted to see Joseph so happy and relaxed, and I looked forward to his wedding day.

Neither of us knew that evening that other matters would intervene.

Shortly after his visit he sent word that the wedding was postponed but gave no reason.

I heard nothing further from him for almost three years.

In other events in those years, King Herod died and Varus moved south to Jerusalem with his legions to suppress a Jewish uprising. The legions prevailed with the usual Roman efficiency. Two thousand rebellious Jews were crucified. I had a chilling moment when I heard the news. Was my friend Joseph possibly involved? Was this why no further word came from him?

Inquiries I made to travellers from the south provided only the information that Joseph no longer lived in Nazareth. Puzzling. No mention of a Jerusalem involvement. Nothing more. Each spring I hoped to see him or at least hear from him. I did not.

In Rome, Augustus divided Herod's kingdom into three parts. Judea and Samaria were to be ruled by Herod's son, Archelaus. A second son, Antipas, ruled Galilee and Perea. The third, Philip, ruled the northern remainder as Tetrarch. Varus and his legions returned to Damascus.

In Judea, Archelaus ruled with an iron hand and issued public insults to the Jews. Uprisings continued in his area until Augustus called him to Rome and exiled him to Vienne in Gaul. A Roman Prefect of the Equestrian Order was sent to rule, a man named Pontius Pilate. He dealt quickly with further disorders.

Eventually peace reigned throughout the Jewish regions, and at last I received word from Joseph. He reported that he and Mary had returned to Nazareth from Alexandria, Egypt with two young sons. He suggested a date when he might come to me and purchase more wood. He thought he might have another buyer for a large cart. Were more wheels available? I immediately sent my message of assent south. I was eager to hear of his adventures and to renew our friendship.

7

The day Joseph was to come I was on watch once the sun rose. He did not arrive until his accustomed time, shortly before midday, and by then I had worn myself down by twice checking the timber in the various storage bins, tidying up my small office in the house, and making frequent trips to the end of the lane to peer toward the turnoff from the main road to see if he was coming.

Because of a special evening menu that I had given my housekeeper the day before, she knew that Joseph was to arrive. She gave me several sharp looks during my pacing about and at last chided me, "Master, you'd best be sitting down. He'll be here when he's here."

Before I could reply I heard the hoofbeat of a horse approaching and the rattling of an empty cart. I rushed to the open door. Yes, he had arrived!

Joseph was unhitching the cart handles from the horse straps as I strode towards him.

"My dear friend, I am so glad to see you," I exclaimed.

He turned and we embraced. As we drew apart, smiling, I saw his countenance was marked by furrows in his brow and around his mouth that I had not seen before, and there was a seriousness in his manner as he greeted me that was new.

"Alexios, it has been too long."

"Indeed. I am eager to hear of your adventures. My housekeeper has prepared a light midday meal for us if you wish to have something before we transact our business."

Joseph frowned. "I think business first today or we might never cease our conversation."

30

"Very well, but perhaps a few details as we look over what you need?"

"Certainly," he agreed as he led the horse to a grassy patch off the lane. "Help me pull the cart to the storehouse."

"With pleasure." As we pulled the cart along, I continued. "I do not know which has been more baffling to me—Egypt, two sons, or that you married a woman, but sent no notice to me."

"All in good time, my friend. I have my first commission for a boat hull for Galilean fishermen and possibly a second."

"Cedar is the best by far. Wood that does not rot in water and also repels insects that bore."

"So I have heard. This is my first boat. I want the seams to be water tight."

"Certainly, certainly. I have more than enough cedar, aged just the right amount for special cutting and leveling. I will gladly loan you tools to help in construction."

It was not until we had examined the cedar logs and calculated which ones would serve well that I ventured other questions.

"So. You are a married man."

"Yes."

"She is the one you spoke of?"

"Yes, Mary of Cana. The rabbi's daughter."

"Ah. And two sons already!"

"We both are set on a large family."

"She is agreeable to your mother?"

"We have arrived only recently. My father died before my return and my mother is not in good health, but it appears things are going well enough."

"And Egypt? What took you there?"

I gave him a questioning look, but he turned away to assess the timbers in another bin for oak.

"I could use some of that as well," he mused. "The stonemason in Nazareth is building three new houses and I need beams to support the upper floors."

"Egypt?" I repeated.

He turned to me with a smile.

"My friend, all in good time. I want to see the latest large wheels you have cut. I have questions about more wood—to the limit my poor horse can pull a long cart. I wish I possessed one of the huge carts! And I need your help with the tools to cut the wood properly. I gladly will pay for the tools."

"Please regard what I can give or lend as a homecoming gift."

"Thank you, Alexios. I am very grateful."

And thus the day focused on the latest work for Joseph, who had arrived home with wife and sons only a few weeks earlier.

Much later, after the evening meal, he spoke at last of what had transpired after his previous visit three years before.

8

The housekeeper had finished cleaning up and we were settling into our comfortable chairs. The fire in the hearth had been lit. I poured two cups of wine, handed one to Joseph, and sat. We regarded each other.

"Enough," I stated firmly. "Unless you want me to toss and turn in my bed, it is time for an account of these past years."

"Perhaps we should wait until morning."

"What! Wait until morning!" Then I realized he was teasing me. "I have half a mind to thrash you!"

"You'd never win. I'm younger and stronger."

"Oh? Did you wrestle with tree trunks in your sojourn?"

He laughed. "No, but I did find work in Alexandria. Carving panels for the doorway of a fine palace and other carpentry."

I attempted a mock glare. "That's the end of the story. I want to hear the beginning and why I received no notice of your wedding. You promised."

He took a sip of wine and set the cup on a side table.

"That part is simple. There was no wedding."

"What!"

"Something came up and my Mary went to Jerusalem to help a kinswoman who was with child."

"And when she returned? Then there was a wedding?"

"Did you hear about the special census at that time?"

"Refresh my memory."

"Simple enough. It was a registration of present-day descendants of the ancestral tribes. Mine took place in Bethlehem, and I went to represent not only myself but also my father, who was too infirm to travel."

"Ah, another tax scheme no doubt."

"Possibly. There were widespread rumors that it had more to do with possible uprisings by younger members of the old tribes. It was a time when Herod was suspicious of all those around him and thought some were forming alliances along old lines."

"You went to Bethlehem in Judea. And your non-wife?"

"As she was nearby, I met her and we traveled together the short distance."

"Please continue. I am enjoying this puzzle."

"In Bethlehem she bore her first-born, whom we named Jesus. The second one, born in Alexandria, is James."

He took another sip of his wine and fell silent, gazing at the floor. I waited but he said nothing more. He seemed to be growing tense and reluctant to continue the line of conversation.

I prompted him. "The first-born. She was with child for some time."

"Yes." Joseph did not lift his gaze to mine.

"You did not marry beforehand?"

"No."

"Ah." I thought carefully before speaking my next words. "She went to be with her kinswoman and stayed on so that there would be little scandal back home about the rabbi's daughter."

"Yes." He looked at me with no expression in his eyes. "And we did marry. In Bethlehem."

"Are you the father of her first-born?"

He was silent.

"The boy. Jesus."

Joseph spoke evenly. "She is an honorable woman and a loving mother to both sons."

"You are not the father of Jesus?"

He was silent.

I sighed and sipped my wine. "I will not press you."

"Thank you. I trust her."

"But why the exile to Egypt for a time?"

Joseph's eyes met mine. "Surely you have heard of the madness in Bethlehem in the last days of Herod."

"Something, yes. But for you?"

"Soldiers were coming from the garrison to kill young children. Herod had a conviction that among them was one who would grow and gain power to challenge his rule. We fled just in time. Thirty or more infants were slaughtered in Bethlehem. I had distant family connections in Alexandria and I knew I could find work there. A place of safety. Time passed. Another son was born, James. Word came that Herod had died and Archelaus was deposed. We returned."

I sipped again from my cup, considering what he had told me.

"My friend, you give me a concise summary and are remarkably composed. I can scarcely imagine my own feelings if the woman to whom I was betrothed was bearing the child of another. I am surprised you went forward with the relationship. The girl's absence for a time in self-imposed exile would have made a natural break."

"Yes."

I waited but he was silent.

"Joseph," I said softly. "There is something here I cannot understand. You continued with the relationship but give no explanation."

"There is no explanation that will satisfy your curiosity. Things have worked out as well as possible. That is enough."

"Joseph, please! Do not think me a prosecutor!"

"It is my business after all."

"Of course."

"I did have strong feelings at the time, I assure you."

"Please, let us pass on to another topic."

We lapsed into silence, both of us gazing at the fire in the hearth. A knot in one of the logs made a popping sound. Joseph stirred in his chair.

"Oh, I was angry at the time. Mary and her parents came to see us just after my last visit to you. I thought it was to be about some insignificant detail. Not so. I was finishing up in the workroom at the other end of the house when they arrived. At last my mother came to me full of venom about what she had just learned. Mary had told a story that defied belief.

"As my mother spoke I was filled with the rage of betrayal. I sent my mother ahead of me so that I might speak calmly when I, too, met them.

"My temper cooled as I passed through the house. It was a young woman's terribly unfortunate downfall. The betrothal could be broken quietly; we lived in separate villages. But when I entered the room where the others had gathered, her eyes were on mine. I questioned her. She answered firmly and her eyes never wavered from mine. I decided to go ahead with the arrangement."

He paused. I waited but he did not continue. His gaze remained on the logs in the hearth.

"She must have a steady head and a winning way to convince you," I remarked. "But you did not marry immediately, as others might have done in such a situation."

"No. Her kinswoman, wife of a priest at the Temple, truly needed someone to come."

"And you had no thought of seeking reparations from the father of the child."

He turned to me. The muscles in his face relaxed and he smiled for the first time. "No. The thought did not arise."

"You proceeded to claim her as your wife?"

"Yes."

Again we lapsed into silence. I was frustrated with our conversation.

At last I drank my wine down and stood.

"You have chosen your course, Joseph, and I wish you well. An abundance of wine at our meal has made me sleepy. I have more woodworking counsel to share with you in the morning, so I bid you good rest for the morrow."

He rose also and took my hand in his.

"Thank you, Alexios. I wish you a restful night also."

"To be hoped. I may dream of this puzzle you have related."

"There is no worth to that. All has come round well."

I gave him my congratulations and went to my room.

In the morning, we ate simply. There was no mention of the previous evening's conversation. The cart was loaded and I helped him to hitch its handles to the pony's traces.

At last we faced each other and embraced. I leaned back while we still held each other.

"My friend, you seem much older now," I said softly. "Our conversation of last evening continues to puzzle me. When you are ready, I hope you will tell me more."

"Possibly," he replied.

We stepped apart, and he swung up to sit astride the horse. He looked down at me and smiled.

"I have a growing family and there is much work to be done to support them. This year I will return in the autumn for more large wheels and other wood."

"Good," I replied. "You are always welcome."

With a final wave from him that I returned, he circled round and began his way along the lane to the main road. I watched him go until he was out of sight.

9

Joseph indeed did return in the autumn. He seemed edgy as we discussed different woods for the projects he would begin during the winter months in addition to another huge cart. Of personal matters, he only said that Mary was expecting again and she was hoping for a daughter.

I sensed that he was deliberating within himself about the content of the dialogue we might have after the evening meal. At our spring meeting he had agreed to tell me more, but I kept my own silence on the matter in our conversation during the day.

We ate silently in the early evening, and then made our way to the usual chairs. Although the days were warm, the evenings cooled quickly and there was a low fire in the hearth.

We sipped from our cups of wine. Our usual companionable silence was missing; there was a tension between us.

At last Joseph looked directly at me. "In the spring I agreed to tell you more about the events that led to a later marriage and our sudden flight from Bethlehem to Egypt."

"Yes," I murmured. "But you said 'possibly.' Please do not feel pressured."

He gave me a tight smile. "I am aware of your beliefs—or should I say disbeliefs. The nature of the events was such that I fear I may become an object of ridicule for you."

Frankly, I was astonished. "Never!"

"So you say now. In the telling, however . . ."

His voice drifted off and his gaze turned to the fire.

I attempted to reassure him. "In the telling I promise to remain silent until you have said all that you wish."

"Very well," he answered and then did not speak for several minutes. At last he began in a low tone, his eyes still on the fire in the hearth.

"Mary and her parents came to see my parents and me. I was finishing up a set of cart wheels. A farmer was to call for them the next day. My parents greeted them and they sat around the meal table at the other side of the house. The length of my delay led to the matter of concern being raised."

"And it was not a small matter," I murmured.

He looked at me. "You promised."

I placed a hand over my mouth and nodded. Joseph's gaze returned to the fire.

"My mother came through to the workshop and related to me the essentials of what had been said. Mary told of being visited by a messenger of the Lord; she was to have a special son; the messenger laid his hands on her head and prayed; she was pregnant."

Silence. He glanced at me.

"That sums it up," he said. "A messenger of the Most High. Not a story to go down well with even the least devout Jew. Blasphemy is what it is called.

"My mother was furious. She could not believe what she heard. Even more absurd, Mary's father, the rabbi, backed the story. Mother was beside herself and insisted to me that the betrothal was broken and the girl needed to go to the man who had committed this vile act. To continue with the arrangement would bring shame on our family once the sorry tale became known. We would be the laughingstock of Nazareth and business would be ruined." Again his gaze returned to the fire. "That was the point she repeated several times. The heritage of generations of carpenters would be cast into the mud and we would be reduced to penury."

I stifled my questions and he again was silent for a time except to say, "Mother was right. That might have happened."

I rose and repositioned the logs. A flame flared up and then settled. I sat. Joseph would not meet my eyes.

"I, too, was outraged," he said in a low tone. "A verse from the writings of Qoheleth kept repeating in my mind, 'God made human beings straightforward, but they have devised many schemes.'"

Glancing at me, he saw my bewilderment. "The Teacher, thought to be King Solomon of old."

Again he dropped his gaze. "Mary, who had so many excellent qualities, had deceived me with another man. Mother returned to the far room. Slowly I made my own way there. As I walked I thought of the Mary I had visited. I contemplated a future for her that now was ruined by one mistake and her own fanciful tale. I did not wish that awful future for her. Perhaps the man had forced himself on her and she was too ashamed—or too frightened—to tell the truth. I would nullify the betrothal covenant quietly and we would go our separate ways.

"At last I pushed aside the doorway curtain to our dining area and glanced around. Mary's mother was weeping. Her father was very pale. Mother, frowning, was sitting erectly on her chair with her arms crossed against her chest. My father was smiling genially for some reason. And then there was Mary. Rather than appearing to be an abject, remorseful penitent, her face was set into a hard mask.

"I looked directly at Mary, who did not avoid my eyes on her. She held her hands clasped tightly in her lap as I addressed her.

"'Mary,' I said as calmly as possible, 'this account that my mother reports to me is a strange one indeed. You are young and as yet not acquainted with the ways of the world.'

"I paused. Our eyes remained locked, her head held high.

"For a moment I was at a loss for words, confronted as I was by her demeanor. Very well, then. I decided to press the matter directly.

"'Mary, do you swear by the Lord that you have spoken truly?'
"'Yes.'
"'You swear by the Lord that you have been with no man?'
"'I do. No man.'

"I glanced at my parents. My father was beaming at Mary. He obviously had not understood what had been said. My mother leaned forward and spoke, hissing the words like sharp knives. 'An inspection will show the truth of this sorry tale.'

"I raised a hand to silence her. She gave a snort of disapproval and settled in her chair.

"I looked directly at Mary. 'When my mother told me of your words, anger rose up in me at your treachery. I could not bear to face you again, such was my rage. But I told my mother I would come here to see you and your parents face to face. As I crossed to this room, my anger cooled. You are young. I do not wish your life to be ruined. I thought the answer was to end the betrothal quietly and we go our separate ways in Nazareth and Cana. Such things are rare but not unheard of.'

"I ran a hand through my hair. 'But you have sworn by the Lord. You are a rabbi's daughter and you know what that means.'

"'Yes,' she replied evenly.

"'Alexios,' I then said, 'I cannot believe the Lord acts in the way you describe.'

"Another snort came from my mother.

"'Yet you have told my parents and now me that the Lord has done just that.'

"I paused and there was a mutter from my mother. I raised my eyebrows as I looked at her. When she said nothing more, my gaze returned to Mary.

"'Yes,' Mary affirmed.

"By now our eyes were staring into each other's souls. The room was still except for her mother's steady weeping. I spoke at last.

"'I cannot comprehend what has happened. It is a test of faith.'

"'Yes,' she replied. Neither of us blinked during the silence between us.

"'It seems I must trust you,' I said at last.

"'Yes,' she replied again.

"My eyes were on hers for another long moment. At last I nodded. 'Very well.'

"I looked at her parents and mine. 'I do not wish the betrothal covenant to be broken. I will honor it and pay the bride-price myself.'

"Mary's mother's weeping ended with a choked sob. She reached over and took her daughter's hand. Her father let out a long sigh of withheld breath.

"Scowling, my mother hugged herself more tightly. I said to her, 'There will be no gossip, Mother. Not a word outside this house. This is my command. Do you understand?'

"She muttered, 'As you wish, my son.'

"My father gave me a huge smile and slapped his hands on the table. 'Good!' he said. 'Now that that's settled, I'm off to the garden again.' He stood. 'Imagine! A messenger from the Lord!'"

Joseph stopped. Now that he had spoken he relaxed.

"That is what happened?" I asked gently.

"Yes."

"You were decided?"

"Yes. Shortly thereafter she went to her kinswoman, Elizabeth. After that child was born, a son who was named John, we met in Jerusalem and journeyed a brief distance to Bethlehem, where our child was born. Jesus."

"Did you ever speak of that day with her again?"

"No."

We both gazed at the fire in the hearth. I knew he was waiting for some response from me. I thought carefully, examining in my mind the sparse details of the story.

"What you tell me of her demeanor—she felt no need for apology to you?"

"None whatsoever."

"Where did this alleged incident occur?"

"In the garden of her parent's house in Cana."

"Did this messenger of your God penetrate her in any way?"

"No. She said he only laid his hands upon her head."

We shared another period of thoughtful silence.

At last I asked, "Have you ever heard of such a thing in your own setting?"

"Never."

"The boy. Jesus. Is he different from other children?"

"He chatters now like other young children. He runs about and laughs or cries as do others."

"No special difference."

"No."

I drained my wine cup. "Well, then, time will tell. You may have a son who will be more than a carpenter—perhaps a great rabbi, or a mighty general who will rid your land of Roman rule."

"Possibly. Thank you for not laughing."

"It is a strange tale, but you believe her and that is what counts. From what she told her parents and you, she seems to be a person not easily duped."

"No."

"And she is kind to the boy?"

"Equally to Jesus and to James. Of course, a mother may at times favor her first-born."

"Despite everything, you find it easy to be with her?"

Joseph smiled. "She sometimes has a mind of her own, as do I."

"Do the differences last long?"

"We are still able to comfort each other, if that is your question."

"Then, my friend, you have a marriage that is blessed."

Joseph nodded. "As long as you are receptive to my account, there is another thing."

"Yes?"

"The messenger told her that the child is a new beginning."

I turned away to hide my eyes. In our rejoicing under the cypress tree, my dear Sophia had exclaimed much the same to me about our child to come. "It is a new beginning!"

"Alexios?"

I wiped my moist eyes and turned back to him. "A sudden memory of Sophia. I suppose every child represents a new beginning. If we are wise enough to understand."

"Yes."

After a few more words we went our separate ways to bed.

10

The years passed quickly and my friend's family grew in size. A son named after his father, Josa, 'Little Joseph,' joined Jesus and James, and Joseph delighted to tell me of their exploits during his visits.

Those were daytime remarks. Our evening conversations often concerned more serious matters, and in those dialogues my respect for Joseph grew. As I look back, I realize that the turning point occurred in his telling me about Mary, and, when hearing the tale, I did not ridicule him.

We still held to our own viewpoints, of course. But visit after visit Joseph opened to me a thirst for justice and righteousness that I saw in no other man with whom I had dealings. His thirst was based on traditions and scripture within his own community, though he applied them to all people.

After our evening meal on one visit, I related to him the plight of a nearby farmer who had a section of land greatly desired by an adjoining farmer who had connections in high places. One night the second farmer knocked down the simple fences surrounding the section and took possession, claiming to have discovered a deed from years past.

Arguments ensued and the first farmer took the second to court. The suit was thrown out and the deed, which most everyone in the area deemed a clumsy forgery, was upheld. The farmer appealed to a higher court with no success and finally to a tribunal in Damascus, which refused to hear the suit.

When I ended the story, I shrugged. It is the way of the world, I said. But Joseph was frowning.

"A pity there was no mediator at hand before the matter escalated into mutual animosity."

I stared at him. "Obviously there was not."

He sighed. "This is an example of the injustice that occurs when the higher laws of God are not observed."

"But Joseph, Syrians? How do the laws of your deity apply to us?"

"My people are called to be a light to the nations. All people are subject to the higher laws of the Lord!"

"Please, calm yourself. What happened is common here and in many places. People of wealth and connections always win out over the little man."

"Is that what you think?"

"Of course. Those in power or wealthy always want more. And they usually get it."

"That is not the standard to which the Lord calls us."

"Joseph, Joseph," I exclaimed, waving my hands at him. "Your Lord sets an impossible standard so that your people are forever failing and must appease him with sacrifices!"

Joseph was silent. At last he spoke.

"It is not impossible. An example. In olden times there was one man who was a judge over Israel. The people cried out for a king, as in other nations, so a man named Saul was anointed. The judge, Samuel, retired in his old age. But first he called the leaders of the people together and gave a farewell speech. The words were written down and preserved. When I was younger and heard them recited by my rabbi, I had him repeat the words several times so I could remember them."

Joseph's gaze lifted to the ceiling. When he continued, his voice deepened.

"'Here I am,' said Samuel. 'Testify against me before the Lord and before his anointed. Whose ox have I taken? Or whose donkey have I taken? Or whom have I defrauded? Whom have I oppressed? Or from whose hand have I taken a bribe to blind my eyes with it? Testify against me and I will restore it to you.' And the people replied as one, 'You have not defrauded us or oppressed us or taken anything from the hand of anyone.'"

Joseph's gaze returned to me. "That is an example of the laws of the Lord which apply to all people."

"Perhaps for the Jews."

He persisted. "For all people. As one of our prophets said long ago, 'The people who walked in darkness have seen a great light; those who lived in a land of deep darkness, on them light has shined.' I believe this to be possible for all people."

I fidgeted. "The ways of man, as you have said, are notable for devising schemes."

"Certainly. Your local farmer was victim of such a scheme—which extended to the highest tribunal. But to any honest man it is a story of disgraceful behavior at all levels and to be condemned."

"I would fight for my land if someone wished to seize it."

"Can you not band together with others and join the farmer in his protest?"

"There are too many difficulties. As I said, it is the way of the world."

Joseph's eyes flashed. "Very well, Alexios. Let me tell you a story."

I had grown accustomed to his stories by then and simply nodded for him to continue.

"Before Rome was founded there was a king who ruled the ten northern tribes in my land. His name was Ahab, the son of Omri. His father taught him evil ways so that Ahab came to power with no understanding of doing justice or loving kindness or walking humbly with his God."

"Yes, yes, I remember your touchstone."

Joseph smiled. "Yes. And in the king's desire for protective alliances he went so far as to marry a foreign woman from a family who worshiped other gods. Her name was Jezebel. In her honor he built a temple to her god, Baal, on the holy mountain of Samaria, and he worshiped that god. He also built many altars throughout the land in honor of Asherah, the mother goddess."

"And the connection to my tale of injustice?"

"There was a man named Naboth who had a beautiful vineyard near King Ahab's palace. The king often would walk out on a terrace of the palace in the cool of an evening and delight in the beauty of Naboth's vineyard. So much so that he deeply desired it and sent word to the owner that wanted it. He would give Naboth another vineyard or purchase it. But the vineyard had been in Naboth's family for generations and he refused an exchange or purchase."

"And the king was angry at the refusal," I suggested.

"He was a weak man. Rather than angered he was downcast and spoke to his queen about his deep disappointment."

"Jezebel."

"Yes. She told him to leave the matter with her. She found two witnesses who would testify that they had heard Naboth curse Baal and the king. Following this testimony before a great crowd, the people gathered stones and Naboth was stoned to death."

I was stunned. "This terrible thing truly happened?"

"Yes. But there is more. Elijah, a great prophet of Israel with the holiest of names, confronted King Ahab and spoke the word of the Lord. For what he and Jezebel had done, wild dogs would one day lick up his blood in the place where Naboth died, and wild dogs would eat the corpse of Jezebel. Both things came to happen."

We were silent for a time. At last I spoke.

"King Ahab was one of your people, evil and misguided though he was. But the farmer who suffered recent injustice is Syrian. How does your story that warns of injustice apply to him?"

"I believe in the one true Lord over all the earth. Through this Lord everything in creation is connected. The Lord's holy name was revealed to Moses, who then was sent to bring the Hebrew slaves out of Egypt into a land of milk and honey."

"And what is the name of this Lord?"

"It is the holiest of names and not to be spoken aloud. When the name occurs in scripture read aloud in the synagogue, it is spoken as 'the Lord.'"

"I have heard talk of your God. I must tell you that there are those who mock your people for their strong belief that they are the Chosen of God."

Joseph sighed. "Yes, I have heard such talk. But we are chosen to witness to the nature of the one true God rather than to assume an arrogant posture about our own specialness."

He leaned towards me. "You do not believe in the multiple gods and goddesses of Rome. You have discerned the truth that they are simply projections of human strengths and weaknesses written large. But the Lord God is one, only one, the creator of all that is."

I started to speak but Joseph rushed ahead, his words tumbling out.

"Another prophet, the one I cited before, Isaiah by name, spoke to the people at a time when many had fallen away from true goodness. I have memorized his words as well. 'Ah, you who call evil good and good evil, who put darkness for light and light for darkness, who put bitter for sweet, and sweet for bitter! Ah, you who are wise in your own eyes, and shrewd in your own sight. Ah, you who are heroes in drinking wine and valiant at mixing drink, who acquit the guilty for a bribe and deprive the innocent of their rights!'"

He stopped and leaned back in his chair.

"This man Isaiah," I asked, "is he living now?"

"No. He lived years ago at a time when the Lord had been faithful to the people but they turned away from him. Isaiah's words present the land as a vineyard the Lord has given. The people took the gift but forgot the giver."

"And you believe these words apply to all who justify their misdeeds and call themselves righteous?"

"All people are called to live in the light and not in darkness."

I thought for a moment. "I hear you saying two things. The Syrian farmer was wronged."

"Correct," he answered.

"But at the same time, if I hear you rightly, the land does not belong to him?"

"Of course the land he works belongs to him. It has been so for generations within his family. In another sense, all land is a gift from the Lord and we are guardians of it."

I shook my head. "But my land is my land."

"Are the trees you are blessed with solely yours or are they in some sense a gift?"

"They are mine by birthright, having been planted through the years by my ancestors and now by me."

"And the rain and the soil which nourish them, is that an arrangement by you or your ancestors?"

"No, of course not. But it was the good fortune of my ancestors to choose this particular plot of ground for purchase."

Joseph smiled.

"If a drought came and dried up the soil for many years and your trees died, how would that reflect on the good fortune of your ancestors?"

"Such a thing has never happened in all the generations of our ownership. "

"Nor in Egypt long ages ago. Remember my story about Joseph of old? Pharaoh had terrible dreams and Joseph told him their meaning. Pharaoh heeded him. Storehouses were filled during the good years and the Egyptians were fed in the hard years."

"I remember. It is a story also of why your ancestors moved to Egypt in order to obtain sustenance."

"Yes. My point is that no mortal knows what may happen to our land or our lives in the times that will come."

"I grant you that, but it seems we have moved a long way from the Syrian farmer."

"He was right to seek justice. To deny it to him was shameful. I hope some of you may join him before the authorities so that he may once again be a good caretaker of his land."

I muffled a yawn. "I am glad to hear of this god, Baal. Perhaps worship of that one might protect my crop of trees."

Joseph laughed. "Oh, of course. Alexios, a disbeliever in all gods, turns to Baal."

I smiled "An interesting discussion, though I need to think upon it. Perhaps it is best for us to retire to our beds now so that you may make an early start for your travel tomorrow."

Joseph nodded, and we rose.

"Think of it this way," he said earnestly. "I am a carpenter. For me, knowledge of the way to work the wood is of utmost importance. If I go against the grain, the wood is ruined and I accomplish nothing. Learning the way of the grain of wood is the way to achieve success."

"True, but I think you again are making a case for the cause of your Lord as well."

"My, oh my." He gave me a broad smile. "Am I becoming so obvious?"

On his next visit I was glad to relate further developments in the matter of the farmer who had been ousted from a section of his land.

A multitude of farmers joined forces with him. In Damascus they surrounded the tribune's house, chanting "fraud, fraud, fraud." Local soldiers were called in. They did nothing but stand by; their sympathies lay with the farmers. At last the tribune yielded and the farmer regained his land. The one who had seized the land was let off with a warning. Evidently he still had friends in high places.

When I reported this victory to Joseph, he simply smiled and said, "Good."

11

In one of the years that followed, Joseph came later in the spring. He sent word that a large group of families was going to Jerusalem to celebrate Passover and to view the Temple.

He came later than usual on the day of his arrival, past noon. I insisted that we fortify ourselves for the usual work by taking time for a light midday meal of bread, cheese, fresh fruit, and a cup of wine.

As we ate, I told him of the news that had arrived from the far north.

"A scandalous defeat for Rome. And Varus is dead." I spoke his full name, rolling the syllables. "Pub-li-us Quinc-til-ius Va-rus. Took his own life, they say."

Joseph's eyebrows rose. "Varus—the same man who governed Syria and crucified the rebellious Jews in Judea?"

"The same. He went from us to return to Rome and in recent years was named commander of three legions with the task of consolidating imperial rule in Germanica. His advisor, Arminius, secretly forged an alliance among the Germanic tribes east of the Rhine. While outwardly vowing allegiance to Rome, he was using the tribes' hatred of Varus' harsh rule to prepare for battle."

"And it came?"

I smiled, relishing the account of Varus' downfall and death.

"Yes. Arminius sent a messenger to Varus asking for speedy help. He claimed that the tribes were rebelling."

"But in truth they were not?"

"Oh, yes. They were united and preparing to ambush the legions in the swamps of the Teutoberg Forest. Under the command of Arminius the traitor."

"A place thickly wooded?" asked Joseph.

"Evidently. Far less space between the trees than here with mine."

"So the Romans could not use their usual formations?"

"Not at all. The legions marched single file through the forest in heavy rain as quickly as possible. The line of their march stretched out to a great distance. The forces of Arminius surrounded them and the rainfall was accompanied by a host of lances falling. It was a massive slaughter."

"Did any escape?"

"A remnant. They built a night camp, but it was more of the same the following day. I have heard that only a few escaped to be captured alive. As for Varus, he took his own life."

"There will be retaliations," Joseph mused. "Romans cannot tolerate such failures."

"To be sure. But I have also heard that the Roman Senate has decreed that the imperial numbers and names of the defeated legions—the seventeenth, eighteenth, and nineteenth—are never to be used again."

I leaned back at the table. "Enough of the downfall of Varus. What news of your recent travel to Jerusalem and the new Temple?"

"A wonderful time—and something puzzling as well."

"Oh?"

"It will take more time in the telling. Perhaps I will speak of it after our evening meal. Let us now get to my list of wood needed for the coming season."

After the evening meal, we settled again into the comfortable chairs by the hearth. The day had been warmer and the logs went unlit on this occasion. I poured more wine into our cups and handed one to Joseph.

"I have told you about the death of Varus. Your turn now. Tell me about your adventures in Jerusalem. A large group travelled from Nazareth?"

"Half the families or more," Joseph replied. He sipped his wine. "We were quite a throng on the road south. Others joined us along the way from other villages. A marvelous procession."

"I am not familiar with Jerusalem. There were places that could accommodate you?"

"Nearby, on the outskirts of Bethlehem. A place I knew from previous years—a large field not yet planted for the fall harvest. I made arrangements with the owner during the winter. This year was special, since so many men were going, plus wives and children. The tents and bedding and food supplies were ready when our great crowd arrived."

"Quite an undertaking!"

"Yes, indeed. A very special Passover celebration for many. An opportunity to behold the splendor of the new Temple constructed in recent years on the Temple Mount. Jesus had accompanied me on a previous visit, but all my family was with me this year, even the toddler, Judah. Mary insisted on carrying our new child, Simon."

"Five sons," I murmured. "You truly have been blessed."

"The Lord has been kind," he agreed.

"Jesus was an excellent guide for the younger ones our first full day. He pointed out the various parts of the Temple and spoke of the importance of the porticos around the inner courts. There men would pass to and fro, debating the meaning of particular sayings in the Law and the Prophets. He was so caught up in the excitement of the scene that he lagged behind after the Passover celebration on the last evening by our men of Nazareth. We had offered prayers and then rejoined our families in the space designated for women and young children in the Temple's outer precincts. Jesus wanted to stay on for a while longer. As he was with older youth from Nazareth, I agreed, reminding him of our departure the next morning."

Joseph paused, assembling his thoughts before continuing.

"There was such a crowd at our encampment, with many people coming and going the last night. Jesus did not return, but we thought he was with his village friends in some other part of our encampment.

"Early the next morning, the tents were struck and the families from Nazareth set out on our journey to the north. It was not until we stopped that evening at a resting place that Mary and I became concerned. Where was Jesus?

"I began circling among the gathered families, asking if anyone had seen Jesus. No one had, but I was reminded several times that he probably was with other families still on the road. A hopeful note, but Mary and I had a fretful night.

"There was no sight of Jesus in the early morning before dawn. I questioned several of the youth who had been with him and they said he had stayed behind on the Temple Mount, excited to be able to enter into conversation about holy matters with the men there.

"I decided that I must return to Jerusalem to search for Jesus. Mary insisted on returning also, along with Baby Simon, whom she was nursing. She was adamant and rather than waste further time in arguing, I reluctantly agreed. One of the men from Nazareth loaned us a pony for her to ride, and another family agreed to take James, Josa, and Judah on to Nazareth with them.

"We reached Jerusalem and proceeded to the Temple Mount.

"I left Mary and the baby in the outer porticos reserved for women and strode onward to the inner porticos, where I soon spied Jesus amid a large circle of men. He seemed quite excited to be in conversation with them.

"I made my way directly to him and gave him a hard shake. I was enraged.

"'Your mother and I have been searching high and low for you,' I shouted. 'And here you are, when we thought you had been eaten by wild animals!'"

"'Forgive me,' he cried out. 'I completely forgot.'

"Still holding him, I spoke to the circle of men.

"'We were with the Galilean encampment—a large group of people from Nazareth. I believed my son was with other youth, and only when we broke our travel north for the night did I realize he was nowhere to be found.'

"Several men drifted away, not wishing to be part of an acrimonious reunion. But one, an older man, spoke quietly.

"'We thought he was staying each night with a relative. He has amazed us daily with his knowledge, which he surely must have learned from you, his father.'

"That remark added tinder to my fiery rage. I pulled Jesus out of the circle and growled at him. 'And you, young pup, what do you have to say, yes? Speak up!'

"'I am in my father's house,' he protested.

"Alexios, now I was livid. 'How can you say such a thing!' I said, and I gave him a shake.

"His eyes filled with tears. 'I don't know. The words just came to me.'

"Old memories suddenly stirred within me. My anger vanished. I stared at him and loosened my hold. I wasn't sure of what to do, so I walked several steps away before turning back to him. Behind him men were watching our dramatic reunion. When at last I spoke, it was in a calmer voice.

"'Come, son. Your mother and Baby Simon are waiting.' I gestured toward the outer courts. 'Do not worry your mother one moment longer.'

"I nodded to the men who remained near him. The older man gave me a tight smile. Jesus and I hurried to the pillared entryway. Mary stood there, holding Simon in his blanket. She rushed to meet us, ignoring the frowns of men in the inner courts. She gave Jesus a fierce hug with one arm and then pulled back as Simon began to cry.

"'Child,' she exclaimed, 'why have you treated us like this! Your father and I have searched everywhere for you. Can you imagine how anxious we have been?'"

Joseph paused in his account and looked away.

I was on the edge of my chair, leaning forward.

"Don't stop now! What did the boy say?"

Joseph sighed and looked at me.

"He said, 'Why were you searching for me? Did you not know I must be in my father's house?'"

I admit I was stunned. "That was all? After going missing! Surely he gave you some excuse!"

"The words have since been engraved on my heart."

"Those were his exact words?"

"Words I have never forgotten since that day."

"He spoke without hesitation?"

"None."

I leaned back. "Ah. And that's the puzzle."

"Not to Mary. As we retraced our steps to the pony, she put her free arm in mine and. . ."

I urged him to finish. "And? And?"

Joseph gave me a smile.

"She whispered to me. 'There was a day you trusted me. Today you have been given your assurance.'"

"Ah," I said. We regarded each other. Joseph's smile had broadened but I was puzzled.

"Meaning what, exactly?"

"That Jesus truly is special. He is destined for greatness."

I nodded. "From what you say he seems to have no shyness around his elders."

"Not at all."

"Did you and Mary ever speak of the Jerusalem incident again?"

"Not since that day. We have not been to Jerusalem again."

"Oh?"

"Times have changed and the cost of visiting the Temple precincts has risen sharply. The atmosphere is very different."

We let the matter rest and moved on to the subject of the wood he needed. That evening we spoke of other things.

12

Through the years the conversations we shared—our dialogues as Joseph called them—were a precious time for me. I believe he treasured them as well.

On his visit one autumn my heart was heavy when he arrived. He seemed not to notice as we looked at samples of the lumber he needed for the next season. He cheerfully rattled on about his growing family. Five sons and Mary was expecting again.

Jesus by now was a genuine help in the carpentry shop, as were James and Josa. They had to watch their feet; often Simon would crawl into the shop and play on the floor with the wooden toys they had made for him. Judah avidly watched what his older brothers did. At the end of the day he was given a small broom with the responsibility of sweeping up.

As they worked Joseph would tell stories from the past. He had related the tale of Naboth and King Ahab to them and later on, stories of King David.

"Jesus," he noted, "was particularly upset about the time when King David walked out on his palace terrace and saw below, not a vineyard, but rather the beautiful Bathsheba."

I grunted to indicate that I also had heard of the episode.

"Alexios, he was very perturbed about what the king did to his faithful servant, Uriah, whose sole desire when he was at home on leave from the army was to sleep at the king's bedroom door to protect his majesty from intruders."

"Yes, a famous story. The king told his general to put the soldier at the front line of the next battle so that he might be killed and Bathsheba made an available widow."

"Jesus could not understand it. 'But we are of the lineage of David,' he burst out. 'Are we evil as well?'

"I explained that the prophet Nathan came to the king and put to him a story about a man whose dearest lamb was stolen. King David was outraged that such a thing could happen. Nathan replied, 'You are the man!' and the king repented of his sin. Jesus and I spoke about the story for several weeks."

"A difficult tale for a young man," I murmured.

Joseph gave me a sideways glance as we stood in front of the storehouse bins.

"Alexios, your face is pale and you are obviously thinking about something other than the story of King David and the wood I wish to purchase."

"Today is the anniversary of Sophia's death."

"My friend, forgive me."

"You did not know."

I felt weak and leaned against the front of the bin where we stood.

"Twenty years. Twenty years. It seems like yesterday."

Joseph put out a hand to support me.

"We should go back to the house."

"No. I will be all right."

"This is more than an anniversary. What has happened?"

"A terrible thing in the night," I said. I took a step forward. "Come with me and I will show you."

We left the storehouse and walked along the path to the far edge of my land, where the oldest and tallest cypress trees grow. As we walked, I told him of the strong wind that had come in the night, a wind more fierce than any I remembered. In the morning I had circled through my property to assess the damage.

By now we had come to the clearing that faced the line of cypress trees.

"And this is what I found." My voice was choked with emotion. I gestured ahead.

The clouds over our heads were gray. Along the line of cypress, the tops of many bent forward. Except for one. The tallest tree.

Joseph was aghast. "Sophia's tree!"

The treetop had cracked in the wind and dangled to one side.

"Yes." I replied. "It is an omen, is it not?"

I began to cry, harsh, bitter sobs.

His left arm circled around me. "No, no, Alexios. Her tree is still standing. And now, look!"

I raised my head. Sunlight pierced an opening in a cloud and Sophia's tree was bathed in warm light.

"Not an omen, a blessing!" Joseph exclaimed. "Come. We will rope down the broken part and the tree will mend and grow tall again. Let us go back to the storehouse."

We walked back to the storehouse in silence. Over one cross beam long sturdy ropes were hanging with curved sawing hooks attached at the end. I pulled one down and we returned to the row of cypress trees. I tried three times to throw the hook as high as the broken branch but my strength was not great enough.

"Here, let me," said Joseph. He took the hook and a long length of rope from my hands. Standing well away, he whirled the hook around several times and then with a mighty grunt heaved it high into the air. The hook caught on the broken treetop in the crevice near the trunk. Together we tugged on the rope and at last the treetop broke free and fell to the ground.

Joseph started forward, but I laid a hand on his arm.

"Please, Joseph, one of your prayers."

He gave me a long look before he nodded and took my hand.

"Eternal Lord," he prayed in a strong voice, "we confess the uncertainty of our days on earth and are grateful for the certainty of your love. May this tree grow strong again as a reminder that you are with us forever and receive with joy those whom we have loved. All glory, honor, and power are yours, now and forevermore. So be it, O Lord."

We pulled the severed treetop behind us along with the rope and hook back to the storehouse.

I let Joseph lead me to the house. I was exhausted and lay down for a rest.

At supper we both chewed our meal in silence until at last Joseph spoke.

"My friend, there is something I want from you."

I was too tired for anything more that day and made a weary reply. "What is that?"

"I have heard few stories from you about Sophia. Please, tonight unlock your heart and tell me stories from your treasury of her."

Such a request!

But I did tell him stories that evening as we once again sat in our chairs. A dozen, two dozen, then many more as my spirits lifted and renewed energy filled my frame. Late in the evening when we parted for our beds, we embraced and I thanked him.

On the twentieth anniversary of Sophia's death, we became brothers. I will honor Joseph unto my final breath.

13

The years passed and much of our conversation consisted of talk about the various trees on my land and what their woods were best suited for. Joseph was quite forthright about some of his projects that had not turned out well. And, of course, there was always talk about his family.

He was proud of his sons and delighted in telling me stories about them. He was considerate of my feelings, however. We developed a code. He would say on arrival, "And how is my friend Alexios these days?"

If I were not preoccupied with other matters, my reply always was straightforward.

"In great spirits, my friend Joseph. Now, tell me the latest happenings of your family."

After his son Simon was born, his mood darkened. Much of his attention focused on Simon.

"We must not question the ways of the Lord," he told me early on. He was obviously troubled. The child was born with a leg that was not quite right, visible even as a baby. Mary continued to carry him about for longer than she had her other sons.

"Joseph, Joseph, these things happen. It is an issue of birthing."

"I know, but dear Mary blames herself."

"Perhaps the midwife did not take enough care."

"No, it is the same woman as before, highly respected in Nazareth."

"Had Mary been eating the same food beforehand as with the other children?"

"Yes. She was fearful, however. In the last weeks, she felt no movement and worried that the child would be stillborn."

Joseph gave me a quick glance. "I do not mean to stir your feelings, Alexios."

"Do not worry yourself. I hope the child's leg will strengthen. Tell me about the others and their doings."

"Let me think." He paused a moment. "Jesus is the serious one. Well, not completely. He also has a strong sense of humor."

"How is that?" I asked.

"He memorizes great stretches of scripture from the scrolls that our rabbi lends him. But he also makes up silly rhymes that he sometimes sings as we work in the shop."

"Such as?"

"Oh, Joshua and the battle of Jericho. The words of Balaam's ass. The downfall of lesser kings in our history. The heroism of the Maccabees. Things like that."

"An agile mind!"

"Very. And he is always teasing his brother James, who is conscientious and precise about everything and makes faces at some of the rhymes Jesus delivers."

"Is Josa now old enough to help?"

"Yes. He is good at the first cutting and shaving of the wood. He has an eye for measurements as well."

"And Judah?"

"Cut from very different cloth indeed. I call him the Curious Cat because he is the one who wants to know why things are the way they are. Last week it was the particular limb of a tree in a neighbor's garden. Why does it grow so crooked? Or the nature of rainfall. Why does it sometimes come straight down and other times it slants this way or that. We had quite a conversation about wind movements on that one!"

"And Simon?"

"Prefers crawling about to walking. We have to watch our step in the shop because sometimes he comes crawling past the curtain in the doorway and there he is, in the way again. I cannot fault him. He likes to be where the rest of us are. Of late he has begun to pull himself up by one of the benches, so I have hopes he will be walking soon."

"Each one very different," I noted.

Joseph sighed, "Even more so with Simon."

"My friend, remember what you tell me, 'The Lord will provide.'"

"Yes. Sometimes it is difficult to trust that saying."

"We all are human, Joseph."

"True. But I feel responsible for the children I have fathered."

He gave me a serious look. "I know of your deep feelings about past events. But I tell you, Alexios, at times I envy you your freedom from the cares of parenthood."

Joseph's family continued to grow. In another eighteen months the daughter desired by Mary was born. Elizabeth. There were no problems at birth and she was perfectly formed.

14

One particular story about Simon sticks in my mind. A troubling incident occurred in later years when Simon was age six or so and attending the rabbi's school in Nazareth. Children his age were taught to write and learned about their faith and Jewish history. Of course, Simon and his brothers learned a great deal at home, since their mother was a well-schooled person in her own right as a rabbi's daughter. Elizabeth was now included in the learning and her younger sister would have her turn as well.

The incident had occurred only days before Joseph traveled north for a visit one spring. After his arrival he gave vent to his anger on the way to the storehouse.

"The sins of the fathers visited on their sons," he exclaimed, "a terrible passage in scripture!"

"What on earth has happened?" I asked.

"Simon—two days ago—taunted by classmates on the way home."

I put a hand on his shoulder and we both stopped. He turned to me.

"My son, limping as quick as his legs would carry him. Two boys followed him ahead of a crowd of laughing children.

"'Born of imperfection,' the two boys shouted, pointing fingers at Simon as more children came running from the side streets to see what the commotion was about. I was in the woodworking shop with Jesus and James. I went to the doorway to see the cause of the ruckus. Poor Simon was sobbing and moving as fast as his lame leg allowed.

"'Child of sin,' the two boys cried.

"I ran and pulled Simon forward into the shop. His two brothers shielded him as I stepped back into the lane and pointed a fist at the two tormentors.

"'Go home, you idiots!' I shouted and I waved the crowd of youngsters away. 'And the rest of you, shame on you! Go home.'

"My eyes came back to the two boys, who stood in the middle of the street.

"'Go home, I say. And tell your fathers I will come to see them this evening!'

"They stood there uncertainly, but the crowd behind them was rapidly dispersing, and at last they turned and ran."

I sighed. "Joseph, young children can be so cruel! Did you go to the fathers?"

"I went that very evening, as I had promised. I took along Jesus and the rabbi as witnesses. The fathers were together, and there was no small talk, believe me.

"'Do you remember my grandfather?' I shouted so loudly I could be heard in the street. They nodded. 'Do you remember my father?' Both nodded again. 'And do you know me?' 'Oh, yes, of course,' they murmured.

"'Let us speak clearly,' I roared. 'What sin did my grandfather or father commit, what sin have I committed that can be said to have been visited upon my poor lame child?'

"'Joseph, Joseph,' one of the fathers pleaded, 'the games of children. What was said is unseemly but not to be taken seriously. Mere words!'

"I tell you, Alexios. That got me going!"

"Foolish men," I replied.

Joseph nodded. "My voice rose a notch. 'Words spoken in malice can pierce the heart deeper than the sharpest knife! Shall our sons grow to manhood in this way?'

"They were silent, casting glances at each other. But I was not finished.

"'Yes, my youngest son has a lame leg since birth. How this has come upon him as his plight I do not know. But I wish him to grow to manhood in the spirit of the blessed Isaiah. Surely the

Lord is my salvation. Therefore I will trust and will not be afraid, for the Lord is my strength and my might.'

"I turned to the rabbi. 'Rabbi, you and my son are my witnesses. Do either of you know or have you heard of any sin I have committed to cause the Lord to visit affliction upon Simon?'

"The rabbi and Jesus spoke as one. 'No. None.'

"I turned back to the two fathers. 'The matter is settled then. See that your sons are properly instructed. Good day.'

"We left. Along the way the rabbi apologized, saying that he did not know how his comments on the passage could have been misinterpreted by the two boys.

"I said to the rabbi, 'The Law is our guardian and guide and not intended by the Lord as an instrument for oppression or ridicule.'

"'No, no. Of course not,' answered the rabbi.

"I looked at him and at Jesus and replied in a calmer voice. 'I trust that this is the foundation for your instruction of our youth.'

"'Always,' the rabbi murmured. 'Always.'"

15

On one of his later visits, Joseph was a great solace to me at a time of deep grief.

Andreas, a close friend of mine in the nearby village, died suddenly in terrible circumstances.

He was minding several grandchildren in Demostrate's pool. He was in the deepest part when a sudden cramp developed in his left leg. The pain was so severe that he could not swim to shallow water. Agonized, he called to the young children to quickly paddle to the shore and run to my house for aid.

Two of my laborers and I heard the screams of the children as they ran along the path and we rushed toward them. We reached the pool too late. Andreas had obviously thrashed about but could not keep his head above water. He was floating face down as we reached the pool. The laborers and I swam out and pulled him to shore. We valiantly tried to revive him but he was gone.

A burial service was held for him at the village cemetery. His widow sobbed throughout and tears were evident on the faces of his grown children, his grandchildren, and others who gathered to mourn him. The prayers of our old ways were used, the appropriate Greek gods were petitioned, and he was laid to rest.

Three days later Joseph arrived. He quickly saw that I was in a sorrowful state and we sat on the steps at the front of my house. I gave him the bare details as he put an arm around my shoulders.

"And the worst part of all," I concluded, "is that the traditions my people share no longer seem adequate to me. The prayers, the petitions, the whole business seems empty of any true meaning."

Joseph murmured, "You loved Andreas."

"Yes, as did many others. There have been deaths in the village that were expected. I would feel sad, but this! A tragedy of the worst sort!"

"Yes. Especially of a long-time friend of your own age."

"I have had no calm for four days, Joseph. Does your Lord inflict such emptiness of spirit on your people?"

"We all are mortal, Alexios. Suffering and sorrow are often our lot. We must trust in the love and mercy of the Lord."

"That gives me little comfort. What sort of prayers are customary for your people at such a time?"

"It depends."

"Ah. I hoped you might have one to comfort me."

"I sometimes assist the Nazareth rabbi in such situations. Because I am generally available, villagers also call on me in difficult times of illness. Of late I have taken along Jesus so that he may learn some of the prayers I use."

"Have you something helpful for me today? Here on these steps?"

"Let me think for a moment." He was silent as he thought. His face brightened.

"I am fond of certain Psalms. Here is part of one. 'Be gracious to me, O Lord, for I am languishing. O Lord, heal me, for my bones are shaking with terror. My soul also is struck with terror, while you O Lord—how long? Turn, O Lord, save my life. Deliver me for the sake of your steadfast love.'"

I sighed. "It is true that my bones have been shaking."

"There is a particular Psalm that speaks to the situation of your friend Andreas."

"I would like to hear it."

"Very well. 'Save me, O God, for the waters have come up to my neck. I sink in deep mire, where there is no foothold; I have come into deep waters, and the flood sweeps over me. I am weary with my crying; my throat is parched. My eyes grow dim while waiting for my God.'"

I nodded. "That is more like it. Poor Andreas."

Joseph thought for a moment.

"There are other verses that I would say to those who are ill. You may remember what I spoke once from the prophet Isaiah. 'Do not fear, for I am with you, do not be afraid, for I am your God. I will strengthen you, I will help you, I will uphold you with my victorious right hand.'"

"What do you say to the dying?" I asked.

"There is a special prayer when one is near death or has died. It goes like this: 'Heavenly Father, our help in every time of trouble. May your great name be exalted and sanctified in the world, which you created according to your will. Establish your kingdom; may your salvation blossom and your anointed be near. Receive now'"—Joseph glanced at me, his eyes questioning.

I nodded, "Andreas."

"'Receive now Alexios' good friend, Andreas. May he hear your words of welcome. Come, O blessed faithful. Enter the joy of my heavenly home and rest from your labors.'"

Joseph paused. "'So be it, now and forevermore.'"

We both were quiet for several moments. At last I cleared my throat and wiped my eyes.

"Thank you."

"You are most welcome."

"I find these words more consoling than the ritual we observed at the cemetery. At least one is assured that your Lord hears them."

"Yes."

More minutes of quiet reflection passed. A hawk circled overhead, looking for prey. We both watched it. It suddenly dove into the woods beyond the clearing.

I cleared my throat again and spoke. "You need not worry about me telling your rabbi of this."

Joseph laughed and lifted his arm from my shoulder.

"Good. I don't think he would understand."

"I am grateful that *you* understand."

Joseph slapped a hand down on the step beside him.

"Thank you. Are you ready now for us to examine my list of needed purchases?"

"Of course."

We both rose and began our walk to the timber shed, talking as we went.

16

Joseph continued his visits. We had many good dialogues about happenings in the Empire and closer to home. Joseph was always in good spirits except for one time.

He was so despondent in his greeting to me that I exclaimed, "Joseph, what has happened?"

"Oh, Alexios, a terrible thing."

"Mary—the children?"

"Not in that way. It is a judgment on my own words."

"Please, my friend, a bite to eat and a cup of wine. You must tell me what has caused you to despair."

I led him into the house. He was obviously a shaken man.

At last, after barely touching the food and offering up many deep sighs, he began his tale of woe.

"Alexios, it is judgment on me for my anger."

"Say more."

"Do you recall how I went to the fathers of the sons who showed no mercy to Simon?"

"Yes, a good story."

He sighed again. "Too good perhaps. As you remember, Jesus was with me and also the rabbi."

"Yes."

"And I said to the rabbi, 'The Law is our guardian and guide and not an instrument for oppression or ridicule.'"

"I remember your words were quite strong."

"It made quite an impression on Jesus, and now there have been consequences."

"But I thought you made your case very well with the fathers."

"It is not the fathers; it is my son."

I succeeded at last in pulling the story from him.

A number of years after the incident involving Simon, Jesus was delivering a cartload of farming implements to men in neighboring villages. After the last delivery he paused by a pond near the roadside to eat the midday meal in the packet his mother had prepared for him. Three lepers traveling on the road approached, ringing their warning bell and chanting the usual signal, "Beware."

They stopped at a distance from Jesus, who told his father later that their disfigured and emaciated appearances were truly horrible.

"And then," Joseph's voice lowered to a whisper, "he beckoned them to come closer."

"Why on earth!" I exclaimed.

"He told me they were such a pitiful sight that his heart went out to the three of them. He was seated against a tree and quickly arose and placed the packet of food and a flask of wine on top of a boulder midway between himself and the lepers. 'Please eat,' he called to them and retreated to his tree."

I was speechless. I had seen sights of wandering lepers, cast out from their communities, along the roads of Syria.

Joseph saw my dismay. "Yes, but that was not the end of it."

"There is more?"

"Jesus told me that they fell upon the food and drink like they had eaten nothing for some time. In a short while they finished and one of the men called out to my son. 'Good sir, we thank you and ask your name.'"

"Jesus replied, 'I am Jesus of Nazareth. I wish you safe journey.'"

"And they replied?" I asked.

"Not according to my son. They bowed to him and turned back the way they had come. He was careful not to touch the unwrapped packet or the flask. He used a limb fallen on the ground nearby to dig a shallow hole and bury them."

"A necessary precaution," I said.

"Yes."

Joseph was silent for a few moments. At last he gave a great sigh and looked at me.

"But, Alexios, that is not the end of the matter."

"There is more? Surely not."

"Yes. Early on a recent morning in the gray predawn, I was awakened by the sound of a bell outside the house. Only once did it ring. Fortunately it had not awakened Mary.

"I rose from our bed and walked into the kitchen area. Jesus was there with a burlap sack. He was filling it with apples from the small bin where we keep fruit.

"'What are you doing?' I whispered as I drew near to him.

"Jesus reached into our cupboard and pulled a wheel of cheese cured after the churning. He whispered back to me, as he slid the cheese into the bag.

"'It is an emergency. People in severe need.'

"Without pausing he extracted a long loaf of fresh bread from another cupboard and placed it in the bag also.

"He turned toward the curtain of the doorway that leads to the sleeping area of our children and, further on, to the inner door of the shop.

"'Where are you going?' I asked, befuddled by his actions.

"He put a finger to his lips, drew the curtain aside, and quietly walked onward through the house. I followed him.

"Reaching the carpentry shop door, he opened and walked inside. When the door was closed behind the two of us, I exclaimed in a normal voice.

"'What on earth are you doing, son?'

"'People in need, Father. Come with me and you will see.'

"We passed by the workbenches to the door that opens to the road. I continued to follow as we walked around past the shed where our animals are kept and came to the gate of the long garden.

"There I saw a terrible sight." Joseph paused.

"Yes, yes," I said. "What was it?"

My friend looked at me. His eyes were moist.

"Three lepers."

"At your house!"

"I knew at once they were the same three that Jesus had described to me. Dear God in heaven, what a wretched sight! They were little more than bones and barely able to stand. My son strode to the man who carried the bell and handed him the burlap bag. The leper nodded and said, 'The Lord bless you.' Then they turned and limped away, heading out of our village."

I was trying to take it all in. "They knew Jesus?"

"He had told them who he was, 'Jesus of Nazareth.'"

"What a scandal!" I exclaimed.

"All I could hope was that no one in the village was awake to see them."

"Someone must have told them where Jesus lives!" I exclaimed.

"I thought so as well, but no mention has been made of it in Nazareth."

"Did their leader touch your son?"

"No. Jesus handed him the bag in such a way that their hands did not touch. As far as I can tell, my son was not defiled. To be safe, I made him scrub his hands afterward."

"Oh my, oh my. Did your son give you any explanation for his action?"

"Yes, Alexios, and I have scarcely been able to sleep since that day. My own words returned to haunt me."

"Which were?"

"The words I spoke after the incident of the boys taunting Simon. 'Father,' Jesus said to me as we stood watching the lepers leave. 'Your words: I believe the Law and the Prophets are a guardian for the people of the Covenant, not an instrument for oppression or ridicule.'"

Tears were running down Joseph's face.

"But lepers!" I exclaimed once more.

Joseph wiped his face with both hands. "I know, I know. I tried to reason with him, asking had he never read the Levitical laws. Defiled men expelled from their community because of the marks of their condition of sinfulness. He simply kept repeating my words back to me."

We were both silent as Joseph struggled to regain his composure.

"Were the lepers noticed by anyone else?" I ventured.

"Apparently not. It was before sunrise."

I exhaled a long breath. "That was fortunate."

Joseph nodded. "Indeed. I could see my livelihood vanishing in an instant! And then the rabbi made a comment in the Sabbath eve service. He warned us that lepers were said to be on nearby roads and we should all take special care to avoid these sinners."

"Do you think he knew?"

"No. But my heart was thumping as I heard his words, I feared that all the men near me would hear and turn to accuse me and my son of defilement."

"Have you had further words with Jesus?"

"No. It is fruitless. He is certain that he did nothing wrong and was following my own words."

"Ah, perhaps the matter will pass."

Our conversation at last turned to other subjects. After a quick review of purchases needed, his cart was soon loaded and Joseph was on his way back to Nazareth. On that occasion I did not question his decision to return to Nazareth the same day.

17

In one of the years after Augustus died and Tiberius became emperor, Joseph was elated on his visit in the autumn.

"Alexios, I will need to make two trips for lumber this time," be bubbled over as we greeted each other.

"Business is good?"

"The Lord has blessed me not only with Rebecca, another daughter, but also with excellent commissions!"

On that particular trip he sought practical advice on a number of tools.

"An estate owner north of Cana wishes a set of bedroom furniture. His wife has specified a design for the various pieces, decorative inlays, that call for knowledge that I learned in Egypt." He laughed. "And I have since forgotten. Perhaps you know of someone."

"Perhaps, but first we will consider the woods to be used. Are you clear about them?"

"Yes, yes. I know exactly what is suitable. The interior of the house has been redone with decoratively painted walls in the Roman villa style. The entry hall and dining area have intricately tiled floors with mosaics that depict the adventures of legendary Greek figures."

He paused.

"In addition, I am to build a large double door for the ceremonial entrance to the house and a smaller one that opens inward on the formal dining room. Both are to have inlays that depict the family history."

Joseph smiled. "Some of which is similar to your own history, Alexios."

"How so?"

"The man's name is Hephaestion. He told me that an ancestor served with a general of that name in Alexander's army and took the illustrious name as his own when, like your Demostrate, he stopped along the way."

Joseph's smile broadened. "Unlike you, his family has attended the synagogue in Cana for several generations."

"To each his own," I replied.

The afternoon was taken up by selection of the lumber that he had on his list and it was not until the evening that he showed me the drawings made by the estate owner's wife for decorations on the ornate new furniture.

"She has a good hand," I murmured as we bent over them.

"A high-born woman. And a beauty," he added. "Her husband adores her and wants nothing but the best for her."

"And these drawings for furniture in the family rooms?"

"Furniture for their own bedroom and that of two sons. I did not meet the older son. He was supervising the planting of fruit trees in the northern part of the estate. The younger one was present in the house. He drifted in and out of the room in which our discussion was held. He seems to be much loved by his mother and apparently bears no heavy responsibility."

"Ah," I replied. "Aesop's ant and grasshopper. One looked ahead and the other gave no heed to the season."

"Yes. And here are the sketches for the panels on the two sets of doors."

We looked them over.

"A good draftsman's hand," I noted and looked up. "I can recommend someone for you, Joseph, but I believe these inlays, though intricate, can be carved by you and your sons with the proper tools. Let me show you tomorrow the tools I recommend to you. If you agree, perhaps you can stay an extra day on your next trip?"

"I am prepared to stay on tomorrow, if that does not inconvenience you, Alexios."

"Not at all, my friend."

We discussed the matter further during the evening meal before moving on to our comfortable chairs and other topics.

I lifted a cup of wine in his direction. "To your newborn, Rebecca."

"Rebecca," he replied. We sipped.

"Seven is enough," he announced. "I am planning separate beds for Mary and me."

I smiled. "Not quite such close company, eh?"

He returned my smile. "She observes the ritual period after each child's birth, and we both are weary and fall asleep quickly. But then . . ."

"But then?"

"In the early hours of the morning we can be quite amorous."

"You truly are blessed!" I exclaimed. "Seven children and a wife who still desires you!"

I had never witnessed Joseph blush before but now he did.

"And I desire her. But seven is enough. I have built separate beds."

He grimaced. "Mary never complains. She has a strong constitution but with all the children I can see that she is wearing herself down."

"Can your older sons help?"

"To some extent—the stable and feeding the animals. But I need them in the shop. And I must keep my mind on meeting timelines for the increasing number of commissions that come in. I have high hopes that my estate owner will open a door to Caesarea Maritima and the palaces of the wealthy men there."

"I wish you well."

Joseph sighed. "Success can be a heavy burden. Please, another topic."

I thought for a moment. "The present emperor, Tiberius."

"So I have heard. What do you know of him?"

"Stepson of Augustus through his mother's marriage to the emperor. Quite a successful military man—conquered Ponnonia, Dalmatia, Raesta, and some parts of Germanica so that the northern frontier is secure."

"Sounds like a better planner than Varus."

"Indeed. No military catastrophes."

"There is talk in Galilee," Joseph said, "of building a new city named in honor of Tiberius on the shore of Kinneret, what you in Syria call the Sea of Galilee."

"Sounds like more trade for you."

"Hopefully. I am grateful for sons who can help me with an increase in work. And I have given Jesus responsibility for all deliveries beyond Nazareth. He excels at relating to people and I am hopeful he also can take charge of negotiating commissions."

"Has he encountered lepers lately?"

Joseph grimaced. "Not that I know of. His attention is focused on memorizing scripture as he travels to our customers. James and Josa are much more talented and steady in the shop."

"And Simon?'

"Simon procures odd jobs with nearby farmers."

"Back to Jesus. Will he become a rabbi?"

"Perhaps. Too soon to tell. Though some of the village folk continue to come to him for help with personal matters. They do so very discreetly for fear of angering our rabbi."

"Hmm. Now a change in subject. Tomorrow I will show you tools that will help you with the inlays and other work. Excellent for making the finishing touches that will delight the wife and the estate owner."

"I am very grateful, Alexios. And now I wish a huge cart for my own purposes. Have you cut more wheels from the oak?"

"Yes, indeed."

Our discussion of tools continued until the later hours of the evening and resumed the next morning in my tool shed. I was glad to see Joseph prospering and I was eager to help him in every way possible.

18

The next day we went to the storehouse to select wood for the construction of the larger pieces of furniture and the two doors. The principal wood was to be oak with drawers of cedar for the interior of the many chests and dressers.

After a discussion that lasted through the morning, we returned to a midday meal of bread, cheese and fruit.

We were both weary from our late evening of conversation and I suggested a brief rest before returning to the tool house.

"Then I have something very special to show you, my friend. I want to see your eyes sparkle!"

Joseph laughed. "You have captured my curiosity! I may not be able to rest."

But we both did.

Arising in midafternoon, we proceeded to a smaller building that constituted my tool shop.

I maintained an assortment of small and large tools that I would loan to customers for their various projects. We discussed which ones might be of use in his commission for the estate owner's mansion.

"And now," I said at the conclusion of the furniture discussion, "I have something special to show you."

I went over to a locked cabinet on the far wall, took a key from my pocket, and opened it. Reaching to an upper shelf, I took down a wooden box that almost filled the deep shelf. I brought it over to where Joseph stood by the table and laid it there.

"My goodness," he exclaimed. "What treasure is this?"

"A beauty, hmm?"

The wood of the box was old with age. On one side, a brass hasp held the lid against the contents, and on the other side, a small keyhole assured that the box was not easily breached.

I took another, smaller key from my pocket and turned it in the keyhole. I paused before lifting the lid.

"Have you heard of the Temple of Artemis in Ephesus?"

"Yes. It is regarded as one of the chief wonders of the world."

"Indeed. A woodworker in Damascus who was renowned for his carving skills brought this box to my father. The tools within it had been passed down from an ancestor who used them in the building of the Ephesian's third Temple of Artemis."

I tapped on the lid of the box. "The woodworker was the last of his line, as I myself am now. He was grateful for the quality of cedar he purchased here and wanted someone to have these tools who would appreciate their beauty."

"I have heard of this temple."

"My father and brothers and I visited it when I was barely into manhood."

"An awesome sight?"

I laughed. "Like nothing I have seen since." I raised one hand above my head. "At least ten times or more my height with massive columns on all sides. Huge statues of Amazons framed the high doorway."

I tapped the box again. "These tools were used to carve the inlays on the tall doors. They represented deeds of the goddess. Forty inlays, twenty to a side. The ancestor had carved ten."

"And within?" Joseph asked.

"We were fortunate to visit when the massive doors were open. The statue was higher than the doors and set well back from them. Gold, silver, and precious stones abounded on the figure of the goddess, who is multi-breasted and wears a ceremonial crown. But enough."

I opened the box.

"Ah!" Joseph exclaimed as he viewed the carefully cushioned instruments. "I recognize some of them, but others are new to me."

I turned to one side. "I have some small pieces of cedar here. I can demonstrate how these tools may be used to create your carved inlays for the estate owner's doors."

The sun was setting as we concluded our conversation. Joseph was reluctant to stop.

I smiled. "We must eat. I propose that we look further at the sketches after our meal. I will take the box in with us. In our comfortable chairs we will think which of the smaller tools can be used to make the precise definitions that the estate owner desires."

"I have forgotten my manners." Joseph drew back. "I am delighted—but I cannot—they are yours. Even to borrow . . ."

"They are my gift to you."

"Oh, no! I cannot think of it."

"My friend, your eyes gleamed as we examined the tools and glimpsed the beauty to be made by them. I wish to honor our friendship by this gift."

"Please, Alexios, I thank you, but it is too much!"

"Ah, but I have watched the way each tool fits your hand so well. It will be my great pleasure to think of you using them."

By the time we retired to bed, he had accepted my gift.

19

The years passed. My housekeeper turned over her duties to a daughter, who sometimes brought her two young sons along with her. From the doorway in the storehouse I enjoyed the sight of them at play in the yard.

Joseph still possessed a full head of hair, though it had turned gray now along with his beard. I was clean shaven in the Roman manner and going bald on top. When I rose from my bed in the morning, I could hear my bones creak. I began a quiet search for someone who might buy my business.

Years before, Joseph had finished his commission from Hephaestion. In one trip he himself delivered the two sets of doors and part of the furniture on his huge cart and reported that the estate owner was well pleased. The task of delivering the remainder of the furniture fell to Jesus, who accomplished the delivery in one journey. Joseph had a good laugh as he told me about the sight of it all.

In a later visit we once again retired to our comfortable chairs after the evening meal. During our meal he had spoken enthusiastically of his purchase of a large flock of sheep and a pasture for them near Nazareth. His son Judah was to serve as supervisor of the shepherds.

"Hmm," Joseph murmured as I poured him a cup of wine. "New cushions."

"Yes." I smiled. "Thanks to my young housekeeper. She told me I needed some sprucing up."

The evenings were cooler during that spring and a fire had been lit. We fell silent as we watched the ruddy flames curl around the logs.

"Joseph, you have fallen silent after easy conversation at the table."

He stirred. "Oh, just thinking about home. The responsibilities of having children."

"To me it would be a delightful burden."

"Sorry."

"No, no. Please. Sometimes I think of what might have been, but then I realize that is a fool's pathway. Truly, my friend, I always enjoy your tales of family life."

He was silent.

"Come, come. Something is troubling you."

He gave a short laugh. "How many years has it been since you were quizzing me about marriage?"

"More than we can count on our fingers and toes."

"Indeed. Now I am in a similar conversation with Jesus and am hounded as well as by my daughter Elizabeth. What a pair! My son apparently has no interest in marriage. Elizabeth fears she is facing a life of spinsterhood."

"Goodness! What age is your older daughter now?"

"Fifteen. She has given Rebecca responsibility recently for our milk cow and cleaning the stable. Elizabeth has assumed charge of the midday meal and household chores."

"This suits Mary?"

"It is a welcome relief."

"Are there suitable prospective husbands in Nazareth?"

"That is precisely the problem."

"How so?"

Joseph sighed. "Her mother always insisted that the girls be given an education as good as our boys. Frankly, one of Mary's charms when we met was her own learning. But now our educated Elizabeth desires an equal partnership with a husband, and I know no suitable man of mature age in Nazareth who feels the same way. Quite the contrary, in fact. She considers herself a notch above the available established men in town." He grimaced. "And she insists upon a younger man, one at least in his mid-twenties. I have pleaded with her, but no, she is firm on the subject."

"A difficult situation."

"Impossible in Nazareth. None of the eligible mature men in Nazareth fit her requirements. And there is no younger man in Nazareth who as yet has the income to support her."

"Have you cast your net further afield?"

"Mary knows of no suitable match in Cana, and Elizabeth stomps out of the room whenever I suggest the sons of farmers I know."

"Poor girl."

His face brightened. "At least Elizabeth is not whining around the house this year about her poor lot in life and her father not being able to find her a good match."

We lapsed into silence for a moment as we considered the situation. At last I roused.

"Tell me more about Jesus."

"Although he seems to have little interest in marriage as yet, he may be of some help for Elizabeth. I have assigned him all the deliveries in the larger area in hopes that he may meet a suitable match for her."

"Does he himself show any signs of moving on?"

"Leaving home?"

I nodded.

"None whatsoever. He is not the craftsman that James and Josa are, but he truly excels in relationships with our customers. They trust him, and fortunately that means repeat commissions for us."

"Perhaps I erred in thinking great prospects were in store for him."

"Both Mary and I are eager to see him well-married to a wife who will give us grandchildren in our old age."

"Perhaps James or Josa will be the first to fulfill your hopes."

"James is so particular and precise in everything—I cannot imagine a woman who would suit him. Or put up with him. Perhaps his younger brother will be the first to marry. He is a likable, easygoing fellow."

"And I recall that it is your custom for the bride to live in the house of the husband's parents."

"Yes, yes, absolutely."

"You would need a second floor for an extended family."

"Yes, and I have already spoken to Mishael, a friend of Jesus who inherited his father's stonemason work. Without telling Jesus, he has drawn up plans for expanding our house. Four more sons besides the oldest may fill the house with their families one day."

"May you have a life long enough to see it."

"Thank you."

We considered the fire for a few moments. Another thought came to me, and I stirred.

"Has Jesus continued his interest in holy scripture?"

"More than ever. He welcomes the delivery assignments because on the journeys to and fro he can concentrate his memory on the new passages he has learned."

"Ah. So he yet may be a famous rabbi."

"He has shown no interest, though he does assist the Nazareth rabbi at times."

"Does he continue to have the discreet villagers visit you mentioned some time ago?"

"Not as much. With the rabbi's consent he sometimes mediates family disputes."

We both were silent for a while. Then I heard Joseph murmuring something.

"What's that?"

"Sorry. A favorite verse from the Psalmist that no longer comforts me. 'The heavens declare the glory of God, and the firmaments show forth the work of God's hand.'"

I smiled. "You have issues closer at hand."

"Each child is different. James is always so precise and certain that he is always correct. Last week he even chastised Jesus for a measurement that was slightly off in cutting cedar for a chest."

"Did they argue?"

"No. I was on the other side of the workroom and looked over to see Jesus smiling at his younger brother. He replied mildly, 'There is time to make it right, brother.'"

"Hmm."

"Josa is always nervous about his part of the work. I try to reassure him, but the comments of James can be quite withering at times. And then there is Judah, the cut-up and jokester. He seems to have no serious bone in his body. I will be glad when he is away dancing around the sheep in the pasture and playing tricks on the shepherd boys."

"How is Simon these days?"

"He's all right, I suppose, though Mary hears him crying out from a bad dream some nights. His lame leg prevents him from playing in the games with the older boys his age, but he never complains."

Joseph smiled. "Then there is our princess, Rebecca. She is determined to gain our praise by being the perfect child. No whining, no crying, no pretensions or airs. Always has a good word for others." He looked at me. "Sometimes all her goodness wears me down!"

"You should be grateful."

"Yes, yes. But I am not sure what really goes on in that mind of hers. After my concern for Simon, I worry about how she will turn out."

We contemplated the logs in the hearth and the low flames curling around them.

"There's one good thing that has happened," Joseph said.

"What's that?"

"Mary tells me she has passed the age of childbearing. She suggested we might sleep in the same bed again."

I chuckled. "Have you taken her up on it?"

"Three days work and I had a new bed frame for us. I carved her initials on one head post and mine on the other."

"Good work for an older couple."

He gave me a long look. "Forgive me if I stir your thoughts of long ago, but yes. We both find that sleep is better with another body warm beside you."

I smiled, "That sounds lovely. And are you two amorous once again in the early hours of a new day?"

Joseph's face suddenly became more youthful. "Yes," he replied. He grinned.

20

On what became his final visit, Joseph obviously was troubled. In the storehouse we were discussing the lumber to be purchased for forthcoming projects. His attention wandered at times.

I nudged him. "Something is distracting you."

"Yesterday I heard disturbing news. Disturbing news for Mary."

"One of your children?"

Joseph laughed. "No, they are all their same unique selves."

His face became serious. "Word came from Mary's kinswoman Elizabeth, that her son has left her."

He paused and I mentally searched my memories. Joseph nodded.

"I spoke of her long ago. Her husband was a Temple priest in Jerusalem. She is the one to whom Mary went to help with the birth of her son, John."

I remembered. "Ah, yes. The missing months before you met up with her and went to Bethlehem."

"Yes."

"Her son has disappeared?"

"No, he told her he was going to seek purification with the Essenes."

"And who may they be? I know of no group by that name here."

"Of course not. They are devout Jewish men who have left Jerusalem and other cities. They live in desert sites established to seek purification from what they regard as cooperative relationships of the Sanhedrin and the Roman governors."

"The Sanhedrin and—?"

He waved a hand. "That is not important. Her son has left."

"Has she no other source of help?"

"Her husband, a Temple priest, died years ago. But, yes, she has the company of other widows."

"Why is this disturbing news for your Mary?"

"It seems to be the fulfillment of something. She fears that it may involve our son Jesus as well."

We looked at each other a moment before he gave a short laugh. "Perhaps a topic for our dialogue after the evening meal. But now I am ready to concentrate on my order."

"Very well."

We continued the conversation after we had sunk into the comfortable chairs that evening, and I poured more wine for both of us.

"The fulfillment of something, you said."

Joseph gave me a level glance. "Many years ago I told you something and you did not laugh at me."

I smiled. "More years ago than we can count on fingers and toes."

He did not return my smile.

"What I tell you now is another part of my Mary's story."

"As I recall, I promised not to interrupt."

"Yes."

"Please continue, my friend. I am intrigued."

"Very well. The husband of Mary's kinswoman, Elizabeth, was an older man who served as a priest who cared for the eternal flame in the innermost part of the Temple. One day, as he was in that sacred area, a man dressed in a brilliant white cloak appeared. The man told him that Elizabeth was with child. The priest, Zechariah, though startled at first, could not help but laugh. He and his wife longed for children but none had come for many years. The man insisted, and Zechariah could not help but laugh again."

"Was his wife at that time pregnant?" I asked.

"Patience." Joseph urged. He continued. "The man told the priest that because of his disbelief he would be rendered mute until the child was born. The name given the child was to be John."

My mind was racing. "The mysterious messenger. The same man who later appeared to Mary?"

"Yes. A messenger from the Lord, Gabriel by name."

"Did he appear to this Elizabeth?"

"Not at all. She and wives of other priests were puzzled that her husband could not speak and suggested quite a number of ancestral names for the baby that was to come, but at each suggestion Zechariah shook his head. At last he was given a slate on which to write the name of the child."

"Ah," I said. "And he wrote 'John.'"

"Yes. Not a name from any man in his lineage."

"Hmm. And then?"

"And then his tongue was loosened. He could speak once more."

We both sat silent. I stood and poured each of us another cupful of wine.

"Mary is fearful?"

"She thinks there obviously is a connection between her kinswoman's story and her own. She told Jesus and James about the word she had received from Jerusalem."

"What was their reaction?"

"Very different. I was present. Jesus fell silent, deep in thought. James burst into laughter and said he hoped that was the last we'd hear of John. Our families had visited from time to time and James never liked John. Said something like he was too holy for his own good."

"And Jesus?"

"When he spoke at last, he was troubled that John, for whatever reason, would leave his widowed mother."

"And you, Joseph, what do you say?"

"Mary had not told me the story until the message arrived. I was surprised that she had not confided in me. But years have passed and neither of us have spoken to our children of her own experience with a messenger of the Lord."

"All these years," I mused. "Perhaps the hand of your Lord is moving."

"Perhaps. But even Jesus is perplexed at his kinsman's actions."

We sat silent for a few moments and then roused ourselves to discuss other topics. At last we rose and went to our beds.

If I had known that the evening was to be our last, we could have spoken warmly of our friendship over many years. But our minds are limited and cannot see the future.

21

I am done with my recollections. It is late.

I have written on this lambskin scroll of superior quality for some time now. The scroll is nearing an end and it is just as well.

My life changed because of my relationship with Joseph, who became much like a brother over the years. Perhaps if we had lived in the same village it would not have been so with daily closeness. Two visits a year gave both of us time to reflect on what had been said between us; time to consider what more might be said when next we met.

I will forever be grateful to Joseph for helping me to make my peace with Sophia's death. In these later years I have come to believe as he did that love is greater than death.

After Joseph's passing, I began to attend a synagogue in a nearby town. I am not a member and do not count for the required number for a Sabbath service. Twice a month the necessary number is met for a service held by a young rabbi who comes to us from a large synagogue in Damascus.

Two young men of the synagogue, as young as Joseph was when his father first brought him along on his trip north, frequently travel south. They keep me informed about Jesus. He has left home and is teaching and healing in Galilee. One of the young men actually met Jesus not long ago and is enthusiastic in describing him.

"Taller than most," he tells me, "and easily seen in the throngs that follow him and his disciples now."

I gather that his disciples are fishermen and earthy sorts. I wonder what Joseph would make of that!

I fret about how Mary copes with her oldest son away, but my young informant reports from his visit that brother James now is the master of the shop work, and sister Elizabeth keeps the family finances in order. None of the children have married.

From what I hear, the years of scripture study and listening to Joseph have resulted in wisdom in Jesus that is rare.

My young man of the synagogue also told me recently that Jesus is a modest person whose central theme in his teaching is the love of the Lord for all people.

"In Capernaum I heard him declare that all men are his brothers and all women his sisters."

That is strong language, and I immediately remembered the story of the lepers.

At any rate, I wish Jesus well. As I thought long ago, he has become a strong rabbi in his own right. Others use the title with him but I understand he does not. Perhaps he yet will.

It is rumored that those in the religious establishment now have spies traveling with the throngs. They should fear him. He does not voice a challenge to their ways as yet, but I predict the time may come for a revolt against their hand-in-glove alliance with Pontius Pilate, the Roman prefect.

Enough. The scroll has reached its end and so I stop. I have pinned a note to it for my housekeeper. She will give it to one of the young men of my acquaintance and charge him with its safekeeping.

This evening my heart overflows with warm memories of loved ones: my two brothers, Sophia, Andreas, Joseph.

May what Joseph believed be true. Good can overcome evil. Light is stronger than darkness. Love is more powerful than hate. And what I long for: we shall meet again.

I am old and weary. I rest now. Tonight I may be released from this life to a better one.

Alexios

www.ingramcontent.com/pod-product-compliance
Lightning Source LLC
Chambersburg PA
CBHW060420090426
42734CB00011B/2386